Management Extra

REPUTATION MANAGEMENT

Management Extra

REPUTATION MANAGEMENT

ELSEVIER

eLEARN

Pergamon
Flexible
Learning

AMSTERDAM • BOSTON • HEIDELBERG • LONDON • NEW YORK • OXFORD • PARIS •
SAN DIEGO • SAN FRANCISCO • SINGAPORE • SYDNEY • TOKYO

Elsevier Butterworth-Heinemann
Linacre House, Jordan Hill, Oxford OX2 8DP
30 Corporate Drive, Burlington, MA 01803

First published 2005

© 2005 Wordwide Learning Limited adapted by Elearn Limited
Published by Elsevier Ltd
All rights reserved

Permissions may be sought directly from Elsevier's Science & Technology
Rights Department in Oxford, UK: phone: (+44) 1865 843830, fax: (+44)
1865 853333, e-mail: permissions@elsevier.co.uk. You may also complete
your request on-line via the Elsevier homepage (www.elsevier.com), by
selecting 'Customer Support' and then 'Obtaining Permissions'

British Library Cataloguing in Publication Data
A catalogue record for this book is available from the British Library

Library of Congress Cataloguing in Publication Data
A catalogue record for this book is available from the Library of Congress

ISBN 0 7506 6681 1

For information on all Elsevier Butterworth-Heinemann publications
visit our website at www.books.elsevier.com

Printed and bound in Italy

Contents

Activities

Figures

Tables

Series preface

'I hear I forget
I see I remember
I do I understand'

Galileo

Management Extra is designed to help you put ideas into practice. Each book in the series is full of thought-provoking ideas, examples and theories to help you understand the key management concepts of our time. There are also activities to help you see how the concepts work in practice.

The text and activities are organised into bite-sized themes or topics. You may want to review a theme at a time, concentrate on gaining understanding through the text or focus on the activities whilst dipping into the text for reference.

The activities are varied. Some are work-based, asking you to consider changing, developing and extending your current practice. Others ask you to reflect on new ideas, check your understanding or assess the application of concepts in different contexts. The activities will give you a valuable opportunity to practise various techniques in a safe environment.

And, finally, exploring and sharing your ideas with others can be very valuable in making the most of this resource.

More information on using this book as part of a course or programme of learning is available on the Management Extra website.

www.managementextra.co.uk

Having a good reputation counts

In an age of industry consolidation, deregulation, mergers and collaboration, the focus for many organisations seems to shift almost overnight, making the challenges for managing corporate image enormous.

Increasing competition to attract customers globally exacerbates that challenge. There is also the increasing involvement of investors, for whom the reputation of an organisation is of paramount concern. And finally, there is the demand for skilled, professional employees. An organisation's reputation will also have a major impact on potential recruits.

What sort of image does your organisation have? Can you identify events in the past that have created the organisation's reputation? What contribution do you make towards its reputation? To answer these questions you need to have a clear insight into the meanings that people attach to popular notions such as reputation, image, brand, public relations (PR) and corporate governance, and how this translates into action inside your organisation. You need to understand how your organisation uses reputation to create competitive advantage and how to evaluate the worth of that image to the organisation and the business.

By developing this insight and understanding, you will improve your ability to:

♦ Determine the features that characterise the reputation of your organisation and the trade-offs that have been made to create an image that matches the corporate and business context

♦ Assess the effectiveness of your organisation in creating and maintaining an appropriate image at corporate and business levels

♦ Identify what is being done and what needs to be done to maintain effective brand images for both the organisation and the products and services that the enterprise depends on for growth and survival

♦ Evaluate the value of techniques used in managing internal and external public relations

♦ Assess how effective your organisation is at providing corporate governance and dealing with crisis situations where reputations may be at risk.

1 Image and reputation

Image and reputation are closely related but they are not the same. Here are two aspects that help explain the difference:

Image	Reputation
Is built	*Is earned*
You have to create and promote an image. It is very much something you build to show others.	A reputation is something you gain over time through your actions. It is very much what people see in you.
Is a cost	*Is an asset*
You pay to create it and you pay to project it. The more image-conscious your market, the more it may cost.	Reputation has a direct link to the bottom line because organisations with good reputations are likely to attract more customers. It will also act as a buffer.

Some organisations have difficulties coming to terms with reputation, especially new companies that have a need for instant awareness and sales and so focus their efforts on image building. But for an image to remain credible in the longer term an organisation must also focus on building some substance – its reputation – to back it up.

In this theme you will:

◆ **Distinguish between reputation and image**

◆ **Explore how reputation and image affect the attitudes that people hold about organisations**

◆ **Assess the value of a reputation and consider how it should be managed**

◆ **Identify five different types of image and the interplay between them.**

Creating and managing a reputation

Organisations, like people, acquire complex reputations. The reputation may be good in some respects and bad in others, or it may be that the organisation has a reputation for a particular type of behaviour that is perceived as good by some people and bad by others.

The sources of knowledge which inform a reputation are:

> **Corporate reputations are aggregate perceptions of outsiders about the salient characteristics of firms.**
>
> **Fombrun and Rindova (2000)**

1 Direct experience of dealing with the organisation

2 Hearsay evidence from friends, colleagues and acquaintances

3 Third-party public sources such as newspaper articles, TV documentaries and published research

4 Organisation-generated information such as brochures, annual reports and advertising.

Figure 1.1 contrasts the degree of control that a PR manager has over these information sources with the influence of the information sources on attitude.

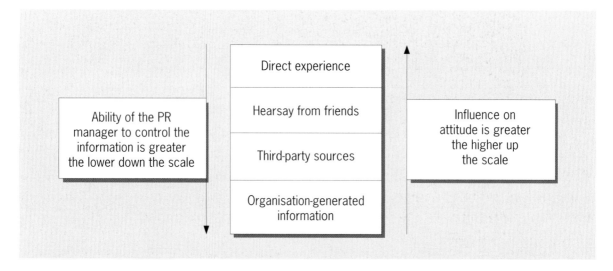

Figure 1.1 *Hierarchy of information sources*

Managing reputation is more than just an exercise in spin. Spin doctoring is a process of putting a good face on unacceptable facts, whereas managing reputation is a process of ensuring that the facts are themselves acceptable.

Managing reputation is about ensuring that everyone's experience of the organisation is in keeping with the reputation the organisation has or hopes to build. This means that everyone within the organisation has a role to play.

How attitudes are formed

Reputation and image both affect the attitudes that people hold towards an organisation. An attitude can be described as a tendency to behave in a certain way towards something. A person's attitude to an organisation might, for example, affect whether they would apply for a job or buy goods.

Figure 1.2 shows how attitudes are formed from three elements:

◆ **Cognition** – what someone knows about an organisation

◆ **Affect** – how someone feels about the organisation

◆ **Conation** – how someone intends to behave towards the organisation.

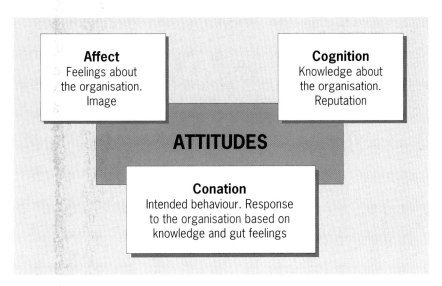

Figure 1.2 *Components of attitude*

In other words, someone's attitude might be formed on the strength of their knowledge of an organisation (cognition), or on a gut feeling (affect), an irrational sense that something is good or bad about the organisation or on a behavioural event (conation) like direct experience of dealing with the organisation.

Reputation describes the expectations that people have about the organisation's future behaviour. It is based on knowledge of the organisation and is the cognitive element of attitude.

Image, on the other hand, is the affective component of attitude. It is the gut feeling or the overall impression that the organisation's name and brands generate in the minds of the organisation's public.

By providing information that appeals either to the conscious, cognitive or to the affective, emotional aspect of a person's thinking, it is possible to destabilise and change existing attitudes.

Skoda was successful in doing this during the 1990s following the takeover by Volkswagen. Having shared with other Eastern manufacturers the reputation for being clumsy, unreliable and old-fashioned, the company was in desperate need of an improvement to its reputation. In order to change attitudes, the company needed first to destabilise the existing attitude and it chose to do so by using the direct route of providing new information. To do this, the company used the advertising slogan, 'We've changed our cars – can you change your mind?' This did not in itself change attitudes, but it did encourage people to question their attitudes towards Skoda and seek out further information. Subsequent advertising has appealed to the emotions in order to build a new attitude.

Activity 1
Assessing current attitudes

Objective

Use this activity to analyse the attitudes of your colleagues and friends towards the organisation. You can use the organisation you work for or another organisation with which you are associated – a club or hobby society would work just as well for the purposes of the exercise. The objective of this exercise is to enable you to evaluate current attitudes within the organisation; in many cases, this will indicate how attitudes need to be changed. In cases where the attitudes might be deemed to be appropriate, the exercise should help you consider ways to maintain those attitudes in the longer run.

Task

Using the matrix provided, analyse the attitudes of your colleagues towards the organisation. You can use the same matrix to analyse the attitudes of outsiders (for example, friends or family members) in order to make comparisons between insiders' attitudes and outsiders' attitudes. You will, of course, need to ensure that people's answers are brief!

Respondent	Knowledge about the organisation's reputation	Feelings about the organisation	Intended behaviour towards the organisation

Respondent	Knowledge about the organisation's reputation	Feelings about the organisation	Intended behaviour towards the organisation

Feedback

Analysis of this type of data is complex because so many different opinions are possible, but it is usually the case that there are discrepancies between the attitudes of members of the organisation and the attitudes of those outside the organisation. In some cases this comes from differences in knowledge of the organisation (insiders often have information which is unavailable to outsiders) but it is also often the case that the corporate culture moulds how insiders feel about the organisation.

These discrepancies can lead to conflicting messages: the insiders in the organisation may say or do things which conflict with the attitudes of outsiders, either reinforcing negative attitudes or raising false expectations.

It is part of the role of reputation managers to ensure that internal and external attitudes match up. This is, of course, only part of corporate reputation management.

Each member of staff has the power to work well or badly, each shareholder has the power to affect the share price, each customer has the power to buy or not to buy. More importantly, each stakeholder has the power to make or break the organisation's reputation simply by saying or doing the right things, or the wrong things, when dealing with those outside the organisation. Therefore reputation management starts with the stakeholders. These include:

◆ employees

◆ shareholders

◆ customers

◆ board of directors, including non-executive directors.

Reputation affects decision making on the part of all stakeholders, so the reputation of an organisation is both created and consumed by its members – see Figure 1.3. There is an element of positive feedback involved. A particular reputation will attract people who feel positive about the reputation and will repel those who feel negative about it. Once inside the organisation, people will act in ways which reflect the reputation. For example, a company with a reputation for treating its staff well will attract managers who like to work in that type of environment and will in turn treat their staff well.

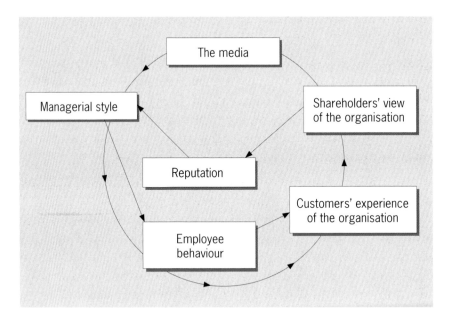

Figure 1.3 *Creating a reputation*

One of the problems with reputation is that different reputations may be attractive to different stakeholders. An employee may be attracted by an organisation's reputation for paying its staff generously, but this same reputation might repel a shareholder. Likewise, a customer might be attracted by a company's reputation for keeping its costs and profits at rock bottom, whereas staff and shareholders might find this threatening. Ultimately it is not possible to please everybody, so managers need to identify who are the key players whose needs must be met, and should seek to establish a good reputation with those people.

In practice, organisations acquire reputations rather than develop them. While it may be possible to re-establish a better reputation (or at least a more appropriate one) this is likely to be off-putting to some stakeholders, even if it is attractive to others. In practice, managers are unlikely to be creating a reputation from scratch – they are much more likely to be tinkering with the organisation's existing reputation to make it more attractive to some people, or to make it more explicit to the stakeholders. Ensuring that all stakeholders are aware of the reputation that the organisation has is important since the reputation feeds on itself.

Reputation and the enterprise

Having a strong reputation pays direct dividends for the enterprise. Research shows that investors are prepared to pay more for companies with higher reputations, even when the risks and rates of return are comparable with other companies in the same industry. Research by Cordeiro and Sambharya (1997) showed that the earnings forecasts made by financial analysts were heavily influenced by the non-financial component of the company's reputation – in other words, financial analysts are aware that reputations have a value in financial terms.

Surveys of MBA students show that they are attracted to companies with high reputations within their industries. Companies that are larger and more visible are apparently better to work for. Part of this attraction is about the reflected glory of working for a well-known company, and part of it is about a perception that working for a major company is likely to be more secure and better rewarded.

The reputation of the organisation is an important consideration for all its stakeholders. Stakeholders are the groups of people who have a direct interest in the organisation's activities and have made some investment of time, reputation or money in the organisation. Because stakeholders have been prepared to make a real commitment to the organisation, their opinions are important. At the same time, these people are creators of the organisation's reputation as well as consumers of it. The main difficulty arises when there are conflicting interests between the various groups – what is good for the shareholders may not be good for the employees and what is good for the board may not be good for the customers. This means that the board of directors often finds itself acting as a clearing house for conflicting pressures.

Even when the stakeholders are in broad agreement about where the organisation should be going, there is likely to be conflict about how it should get there. Broadly speaking, all the stakeholders are likely to want the organisation to be ethical, reliable and even profitable, but each group will have a very different view on how these outcomes are to be achieved.

A particular problem is that of meeting the needs of different market segments while maintaining a consistent image. For example, British Airways (BA) needs to appeal to business-class and first-class passengers because these people are the most profitable segment of the market. This means that BA aircraft have been adapted to provide fully reclining seats in business class – in effect, a bed for each passenger. For intercontinental travel, this has to be a major selling point for business travellers, as anyone who has tried to sleep on an aeroplane can testify. The downside is that this means less space on the plane for economy passengers, and since many intercontinental economy-class passengers are backpackers and the like, this causes a problem for BA's future reputation. Backpackers are seen as a long-term investment by airlines, since they are typically students spending a year travelling before going to university – in other words, they are the future business-class travellers.

Stakeholders' interests are becoming increasingly important in the age of accountability. Failure to take account of stakeholder needs not only damages the organisation's reputation, but can also lead to lawsuits or other direct action. Other sections in this book examine ways of avoiding these outcomes.

Types of image

There are five basic types of image:

1 Mirror image.
2 Current image.
3 Wish image.
4 Corporate image.
5 Multiple image.

Mirror image is how people within the organisation think the outside world sees it. Often those within the organisation, especially its leaders, develop a false impression of what the outside world thinks of their organisation – this can be born of wishful thinking or of self-delusion, but it typically comes about because an unbiased opinion from outside the organisation is lacking. When external research is carried out, perhaps by a PR consultancy, members of the organisation are often surprised and disappointed to find that the organisation's external image is not what they expected.

The **current image** is that held by people outside the organisation and may be more or less accurate according to whether it is based on experience or on misunderstanding and half-truths. The current image is likely to be less than accurate, since people outside the organisation do not have access to the amount of information that people on the inside have. It is generally a great deal better for the organisation to have an accurate current image than it is to have a favourable current image: if the image is more favourable than the truth, a day of reckoning is inevitable sooner or later.

The **wish image** is the image desired by management. Often it equates to a vision statement, defined when the organisation was founded, and is the image the organisation is working towards.

Wish images are not always realised, of course. During the 1960s, town planners in Spain had the idea of creating a quiet, respectable resort for the wealthier middle classes of Europe, foreseeing (correctly) that these people would have large disposable incomes and would be prepared to spend increasing amounts of their money on leisure, particularly as air travel became more widely available. The wish image of the resort was that of a quiet, respectable town with an old quarter at its heart and upmarket, comfortable hotels around it. The result of these careful deliberations was Benidorm – now often regarded as the epitome of rampant overdevelopment.

The **corporate image** is the image of the organisation, as opposed to the image of its products or services. Corporate image is composed of organisational history, financial stability, reputation as an employer, history of corporate citizenship, and so forth. It is possible to have a good corporate image and a poor reputation for products and services, and vice versa. For example, Body Shop enjoys an exemplary corporate image while its products are almost invisible, whereas Rolls-Royce has an outstanding image for its products coupled with a somewhat chequered corporate history.

The **multiple image** occurs when separate branches of the business or even individuals within the organisation create their own image within that of the overall corporation. For example, sales representatives will each have a personal image and reputation with customers which may or may not accord with the overall corporate image.

These five types of image are summarised in Table 1.1.

Mirror image	How we think others see us. Sometimes this image is the result of self-delusion
Current image	The actual view of us held by outsiders. This is not always as positive as we might wish it to be
Wish image	How we wish others to see us. This is usually something to strive for – it may not bear any relation to what is actually possible!
Corporate image	The image of the organisation, rather than the images of its brands
Multiple image	The many images put forward by the individuals working within the organisation. These may or may not be co-ordinated successfully

Table 1.1 *Different images*

Company uniforms

Many American organisations like to present a single corporate image by requiring staff to wear company uniforms. IBM had a corporate uniform for its salespeople (blue sports jackets and grey slacks) up until the 1960s, when a revolt by its French staff caused the company to rethink – but even now, IBM salespeople tend to have a similar appearance. Most IBMers wear dark suits or trouser suits, white shirts or blouses, and conservative ties – although there are no formal rules about this any more, people tend to conform to the company norm.

This is not the only occasion when the French have refused to go along with an American company's plans to make them wear uniforms. Disney laid down strict guidelines on the appearance of its staff (even those who are not appearing as Mickey Mouse). It requires men to wear their hair short and women to wear their hair tied back. At Disneyland Paris the company met with a flat refusal to accede to this requirement and was forced to back down.

Sony put its workers in company uniforms shortly after the company was formed. At the time, post-war clothing shortages meant that many employees were coming to work in the rags of their army uniforms. Akio Morita thought it would improve morale if the workers were better dressed, so he did a deal to buy a bulk supply of jackets and trousers. An unexpected spin-off from this was that because executives and workers were dressed alike, there was a marked increase in company solidarity.

Presumably French workers would have revolted against this as well!

Creating a 'good' image is really about creating an accurate image. PR is not about spin-doctoring or distorting the truth in order to fool the public. People quickly find out whether the image equates well to reality and act accordingly.

Activity 2
The wish image

Objective

Use this activity to find out what the organisation's wish image is. The purpose of this exercise is to assess whether the wish image is realistic and attainable, and (in conjunction with the previous activity) to make a comparison between what the organisation wishes its image to be, and what its actual image is. This will enable you to consider ways of closing the gap between what is wanted and what already exists.

Task

Using available corporate documents, determine what the wish image of the organisation you work for is. You should be able to define this in terms of the components of attitude: cognition (knowledge and thoughts about the organisation), affect (feelings about the organisation) and conation (intended behaviour towards the organisation).

This wish image is unlikely to tally exactly with the actual image of the organisation and there may be differences in the image the organisation wishes to generate among different groups. If this is the case, there is scope within this activity to analyse and record separately for each group.

Typically, the wish image will be contained in such documents as the mission statement, the vision statement, shareholders' annual reports, corporate advertising, corporate press releases and, occasionally, in internal memoranda.

Use the table provided to record your analysis of the documentation.

Document	What the organisation would like people to believe about it	What the organisation would like people to feel about it	How the organisation would like people to behave towards it

Feedback

If you compare the results of this analysis with those of the attitude analysis in Activity 1, you will almost certainly find that there are discrepancies. The problem for any reputation manager is to find ways of closing the gaps between what the organisation wants to portray and what the public actually observes.

You might like to consider what the organisation could do to narrow the gap in perception.

◆ Recap

Distinguish between reputation and image

◆ A reputation is something that is acquired over time through actions and results whereas an image is something that you create to convey a message to others.

◆ Reputation and image should reinforce each other and be consistent. A flashy image, for example, has limited value if it is contradicted by the organisation's reputation.

◆ A strong reputation is an asset, attracting more customers, higher-calibre recruits and more investors.

Explore how reputation and image affect the attitudes that people hold about organisations

◆ Attitudes towards an organisation develop as a result of: knowledge that we gain (cognition), feelings we experience (affect) and behavioural experiences (conation).

◆ Our perception of reputation is based on what we know about an organisation. It affects the cognitive aspect of our attitude. An image, on the other hand, appeals to our emotions – the affect aspect.

◆ It is possible to change attitudes by providing new information that appeals to either the cognitive or emotional thought processes.

Assess the value of a reputation and consider how it should be managed

◆ Managing reputation is about ensuring that everyone's experience of the organisation is consistent with the reputation that the organisation has or hopes to build.

◆ The organisation's stakeholders are key: they have the power to make or break a reputation. They are diverse in their requirements and what is attractive to one group might prove unacceptable to another. Managers need to identify their most important stakeholders and establish a good reputation with them.

Identify five different types of image and the interplay between them

♦ The fives types of image are:

– mirror image: how we think others see us

– current image: the actual view of us held by outsiders

– wish image: how we wish others to see us

– corporate image: the image of the organisation

– multiple image: the diverse images conveyed by the organisation's staff.

♦ The image should be managed so that it is as accurate and consistent as possible.

 **More @**

Davies, G., Chun, R., Vinhas Da Silva, R. and Roper, S. (2002) *Corporate Reputation and Competitiveness,* **Routledge**
This book presents the case for reputation as a strategic tool for organisations in the 21st century. As well as a review of current thinking, the text contains the authors' approach to reputation measurement and management: the 'Reputation Chain'.

Balmer, J. and Greyser, S. (eds) (2003) *Revealing the Corporation: Perspectives on Identity, Image, Reputation and Corporate Branding,* **Routledge**
The book draws on articles from leading journals in the field and includes important recent articles as well as classics, written by recognised masters of the genre, which still inform current debate and practice.

Schultz, M., Hatch, M. and Larsen M. H. (2000) *The Expressive Organization: Linking Identity, Reputation and the Corporate Brand,* **Oxford University Press**
According to the authors, the future lies with 'the expressive organization'. Such organisations not only understand their distinct identity and their brands, but are also able to express these externally and internally.

The **Manchester Business School** has established a **Corporate Reputation Institute**. Its wesbite is at
www.mbs.ac.uk/research/centres-projects/corporate-reputation/index.htm

2

Creating and managing a corporate image

Managing the corporate image is a twofold activity. Firstly, the image needs to be consistent across the organisation. Secondly, it should be possible to maintain the image in the face of outside influences, notably in emergencies and crises.

Creating consistency in the image is dependent on having accurate information about public perception of the organisation and feeding this back to the members of the organisation. Avoidance of multiple images is a concern for many organisations, but in practice the inherent diversity in the workforce makes it difficult to achieve. The most practical approach is probably that of developing a strong corporate culture based around a clear vision statement.

In this theme we explore some of the tools that are available for creating and managing the corporate image and consider the implications of employing an outside agency to help.

You will:

◆ **Explore how the corporate image adds to stakeholder value**

◆ **Explore the benefits and considerations of sponsorship and word-of-mouth communication as image development techniques**

◆ **Identify ways of handling complaints so as to increase customer loyalty**

◆ **Understand the issues surrounding the appointment and control of outside agencies**

◆ **Identify the key factors in choosing an outside agency.**

Corporate image and added value

Corporate image is not a luxury. The image of a corporation translates into hard added value for shareholders. This is partly because of the effect that image has on the corporation's customers, but is also a function of the effects it has on staff, and is very much a result of the influence the image has on shareholders. High-profile companies are more attractive to shareholders, even if the company's actual performance in terms of profits and dividends is no better than average. Since the central task of management is to maximise shareholder value, image must be central to management thinking and action.

Maximising shareholder value is not the same as maximising profits – see Figure 2.1 for a comparison. Profit maximisation tends to be short-term, a matter of cutting costs, reducing investment, downsizing, increasing sales volumes at the expense of long-term customer loyalty, and so forth. Adding value to the shareholders' assets is about creating a secure, growing, long-term investment. Since the dot.com bubble burst, investors have become painfully aware that investments in companies with spectacular profits but little underlying solidity is a quick way to lose money. City analysts look more and more towards using measures such as customer loyalty, brand awareness and investment levels when judging the long-term prospects for companies. Taxation structures now discourage speculation on the markets and the increase in the number of small private investors has resulted in much more long-term thinking.

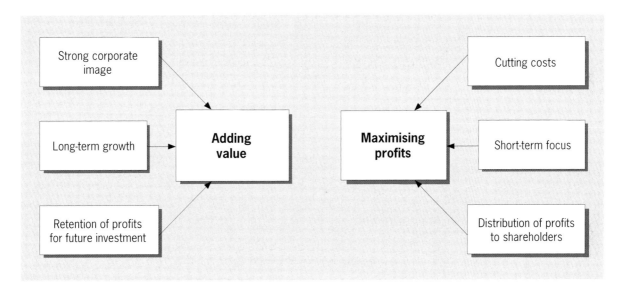

Figure 2.1 *Comparison between adding value and maximising profits*

The counter-argument to this is that the shifting global marketplace has reduced survival prospects for companies. The life expectancy of a company is now less than 20 years (De Geus, 1997). Maintaining a profitable competitive advantage is also problematic. If a company finds a profitable market niche, competitors respond rapidly and profits fall to the point where it is almost impossible to maintain an adequate return on the original capital investment (Black et al., 1998).

Cable TV
The UK cable TV industry is in trouble. In the 1980s cable was hailed as the future for all forms of communication. E-mail, the Internet, TV and telephone were all promised a golden future. Fibre-optic technology meant that a huge amount of information could be transmitted through cables, and streets were dug up all over Britain to lay cables. Future growth was

forecast to be explosive. In Thatcher's Britain the cutting edge of technology promised huge returns for investors.

In the 21st century things look rather different. The investors' original capital has been sunk (literally) into holes in the ground. Telephone companies such as BT have not been prepared to sit still and let the cable operators steal their markets, nor have satellite TV (and even terrestrial TV) stations been prepared to roll over and play dead. Despite the huge growth in Internet access, which has utilised the cable capacity, competition is so strong that the cable companies are now in serious financial trouble.

For the consumer, this is actually good news. If the cable companies go broke, the liquidators will sell the assets off for a much lower price than the original cost of installing cables. The new operators, freed of servicing the capital, will be able to show a profit – but the original investors will lose out badly.

Obviously some well-established companies have maintained their shareholder value year after year, sometimes by using profits to increase capital value rather than pay dividends. Companies with good reputations are regarded as safe investments because they maintain steady growth, even if the dividends are small. Some investors regard large dividend payouts as a sign that the company is buying shareholder goodwill rather than building the business. However, even blue-chip companies are not immune to environmental shifts.

In recent years, business thinking has become customer orientated, on the basis that pleasing the customers is the best way to get their money from them. In fact, customer orientation does not necessarily mean that the company gives its customers everything they want. It does mean that it ensures that customers are satisfied and loyal in order to maximise the long-term survival potential of the company.

The value that accrues from image management has always been accounted for under the heading of 'goodwill' on the company's balance sheet. The goodwill element of the company's value is the difference between the value of its tangible assets and its value on the stock market. For some companies, the value of its goodwill is actually the bulk of its overall value. For example, Coca-Cola's goodwill value is more than 80 per cent of the company's total value. Much of this goodwill value comes from the Coca-Cola brand itself. This approach to valuing a company's reputation and image is now regarded as being somewhat crude, and new measures are being developed to take account of brand value, customer loyalty values, and so forth in order to move away from the reliance on financial measures when assessing a company's success.

Activity 3
Valuing the organisation

Objective

Use this activity to identify the value of your organisation's reputation. The purpose of this exercise is to enable you to evaluate the corporate image-building activities of the organisation, and assess the costs and benefits of these activities. In some cases, these activities will be seen to be of direct cash benefit to the organisation; in others the benefits may well be less clear.

Task

Using an up-to-date edition of the financial press and a copy of the shareholders' annual report, calculate the stock market valuation of the organisation. This is done by multiplying the number of issued shares by the quoted stock market price for them. You need to take account of other types of shares – preferential shares, non-voting shares and so forth. If you have difficulty with finding out this information, you may be able to ask someone in the finance department of your organisation for help.

Now compare this with the corporate balance sheet, which has a valuation of the organisation's tangible assets. The difference between the two figures is the value of the corporate reputation.

Your calculations:

Is the figure bigger or smaller than the value of the physical assets? Is the figure positive or negative? (It is, of course, possible for an organisation's stock market valuation to be below that of the book value of its assets.)

Feedback

In the vast majority of cases, the stock market value of the organisation is greater than the asset value. If this is not the case, the organisation is likely to be taken over by another organisation and in many cases would be broken up and sold off for its asset value – this is called 'asset stripping' and was common practice during the 1970s when inflation was high and profits were low. Some of this extra value is created by intangible assets such as valuable patents or other intellectual property, but much of it is the value of the corporate reputation. Even a fairly casual reading of the financial press will show what the effect of a major scandal is on share prices.

In some cases, the value of the corporate reputation greatly exceeds that of the physical assets, in which case it is obvious that a relatively small investment in corporate reputation building has proved worthwhile. In other cases, it may well be worth considering greater expenditure on reputation building rather than on physical assets – this may be a quicker route to building shareholder value.

Techniques for managing corporate image

Sponsorship

Sponsorship has been defined as:

...an investment, in cash or kind, in an activity in return for access to the exploitable commercial potential associated with this activity.

Source: *Meenaghan* (1991)

Sponsorship of the arts or sporting events is an increasingly popular way of generating positive feelings about organisations.

Sponsorship in the UK grew a hundredfold between 1970 and 1993, from £4m to £400m. It has continued to grow ever since, with estimates for 2001 ranging between £1,000m and £1,400m. A large part of this increase has come from tobacco firms, due to global restrictions on tobacco advertising. Sponsorship of Formula One motor racing, horse racing, cricket and many arts events such as the Brecon Jazz Festival would be virtually non-existent without the major tobacco companies. Organisations sponsor for a variety of different reasons, as shown in Table 2.1.

Objectives	% Agreement	Rank
Press coverage/exposure/opportunity	84.6	1
TV coverage/exposure/opportunity	78.5	2
Promote brand awareness	78.4	3
Promote corporate image	77.0	4
Radio coverage/exposure/opportunity	72.3	5
Increase sales	63.1	6
Enhance community relations	55.4	7
Entertain clients	43.1	8
Benefit employees	36.9	9
Match competition	30.8	10
Fad/fashion	26.2	11

Table 2.1 *Reasons for sponsorship*   Source: *Zafer Erdogan and Kitchen* (1998)

The basis of sponsorship is to take customers' beliefs about the sponsored event and link them to the organisation doing the sponsoring. Thus an organisation wishing to appear middle-class and respectable might sponsor a theatre production or an opera, whereas an organisation wishing to appear to be 'one of the lads' might sponsor a football team. As far as possible, sponsorship should relate to the organisation's existing image.

Sponsorship will only work if it is linked to other marketing activities, in particular to advertising. Hefler (1994) estimates that two to three times the cost of sponsorship needs to be spent on advertising if the exercise is to be effective. The advertising should tell customers why the organisation has chosen this particular event to sponsor so that the link between the organisation's values and the sponsored event is clear. A bank which claims to be 'Proud to sponsor the Opera Festival' will not do as well as it would if it were to say: 'We believe in helping you to enjoy the good things in life – that's why we sponsor the Opera Festival'. A recent development in sponsorship is to go beyond the mere exchange of money as the sole benefit to the sponsored organisation or event. If the sponsored organisation can gain something tangible in terms of extra business or extra publicity for its cause, then so much the better for both parties.

Lincoln and Cirque du Soleil
Lincoln-Mercury (a Ford subsidiary) sponsored a mini-tour of the Canadian circus company, Cirque du Soleil. The tour was linked to the new model of the Lincoln luxury car, but Cirque du Soleil was able to use the mini-tour as a publicity exercise for its later major tour of the United States. This in turn led to more publicity for Lincoln, so the two organisations developed a symbiotic relationship (beneficial to both).

There is evidence that consumers feel gratitude towards the sponsors of their favourite events, although of course this may be an emotional linking of the sponsor and the event rather than a feeling of gratitude that the sponsor made the event possible. The difference between these emotions is academic in any case – if sponsorship leads to an improvement in the organisation's standing with customers, that should be sufficient. There are also spin-offs for the internal PR of the organisation: most employees like to feel that they are working for a caring organisation, and sponsorship money often leads to free tickets or price reductions for staff of the sponsoring organisation.

The following criteria apply when considering sponsorship (Hefler, 1994):

♦ The sponsorship must be economically viable – i.e. it should be cost-effective

♦ The event or organisation being sponsored should be consistent with the brand image and overall marketing communications plans

♦ It should offer a strong possibility of reaching the desired target audience

♦ Care should be taken if the event has been sponsored before: the audience may confuse the sponsors, and you may be benefiting the earlier sponsor.

Another recent development in sponsorship is ambush marketing. This is the practice of linking one's product to a sponsored event without actually sponsoring anything. For example, during the 1998 FIFA World Cup soccer tournament, some companies ran World Cup competitions or World Cup promotions without actually contributing anything to the event. There is very little that can be done to prevent this, although sponsoring companies can console themselves with the thought that the TV cameras at the event itself will focus on their company names, not on those of the ambush marketers.

Word of mouth

People often discuss products. We like to talk about the things we have bought, the films we have seen and the holidays we have been on or are about to go on. We like to ask our friends' opinions and to air our own. This type of communication is extremely powerful as a marketing tool, but it is also difficult to control.

The main advantage of word-of-mouth communication is that it comes from a reliable source. People tend to trust the word of their friends and acquaintances much more than they do advertising. This is perhaps a little strange considering that advertisers are constrained by law to be legal, decent, honest and truthful. Few people can say that about their friends.

Another advantage is that word-of-mouth communication is interactive. It allows for discussion and for asking questions if a particular aspect of the communication is unclear.

The main disadvantage of word of mouth is that it is difficult to control. The evidence is that bad news travels twice as fast as good news, and that most word of mouth is actually negative.

Word of mouth can be encouraged and, to an extent, directed by the following means:

◆ **Press releases** News stories about the organisation will generate discussion, to a greater or lesser extent.

◆ **Bring-a-friend schemes** In such a scheme, a reward is given for recruiting a friend. Since some people feel uncomfortable about being rewarded for recommending a friend to do something, the reward is often given to the friend instead. The Dutch railway system, Nederlands Spoorweg, ran a very successful campaign to recruit more people to its senior citizens' railcard. The company simply sent out packs containing trial-period railcards to its retired workers asking them to pass these on to their friends.

◆ **Awards and certificates** Trophies, certificates and awards are often displayed or at least talked about. The Blood Transfusion Service uses this to good effect by giving donors awards for giving 10 pints, 20 pints, and so forth.

Some people are more useful than others in terms of word-of-mouth communication because they are more influential. Identifying these influential people is not easy, but some general principles have been established.

Firstly, demography has very little influence for most products. Although age might have some bearing on, say, purchase of trainers, it is far from being the most influential factor. Social activity shows a better correlation, since opinion leaders and influencers are usually gregarious. Typically, influencers are positive towards new ideas and are innovative. This is not surprising, since in order to recommend a product one might assume that the individual will have tried it, read about it or taken some interest in it. There is a low correlation between personality characteristics and opinion leadership, but influencers are more interested in the product area than other people. This means that someone might be an influencer for one product category and not for another – again, not surprising. One might consult a computer enthusiast about computers, but not expect the same person to be able to advise about musical instruments.

In view of the fact that most word of mouth is negative, managers might be better employed in trying to prevent dissatisfied customers from voicing their complaints to others.

Three basic types of complaining behaviour have been identified (Singh, 1988): **voiced response**, in which the customer comes back and complains to the supplier; **third-party response**, in which the customer enlists the aid of lawyers, consumer organisations, trading standards officers, and so forth; and **private response**, in which the customer complains to friends. These are summarised in Table 2.2. Customers who come back with a complaint actually give the organisation a chance to put things right before they move on to one of the other two options, so complaints should really be encouraged whenever possible. This is why waiters always ask if the meal is all right – waiting until the food has been eaten or until a complaint has been made is probably counterproductive.

Voiced response	The customer comes back to complain. This is actually the best type of response from the supplier's viewpoint because it offers an opportunity to rescue the situation
Third-party response	The customer enlists the aid of a bigger, more powerful ally such as a lawyer or a consumer protection organisation
Private response	The customer tells everybody else about the problem. This could well be the worst outcome for the supplier

Table 2.2 *Types of complaining behaviour*

In the case of a physical product, simple replacement of the faulty item is the usual remedy for a complaint. In service industries, the situation is more complex because services are difficult to replace. In general, services fall into three categories as regards redress for complaints (Blythe, 1997):

1 Services where it is appropriate to offer a repeat service or a voucher – dry cleaning, domestic appliance repairs and takeaway food are examples.

2 Services where a refund is sufficient – retail shops, cinemas and theatres, and video rental shops are examples.

3 Services where consequential losses might have to be compensated for – examples are legal services, medical services and hairdressers.

The key factors in deciding how to handle the complaint are the strength of the complaint, the degree of blame attaching to the supplier (from the customer's viewpoint) and the legal and moral relationship between the supplier and the consumer. Failure to handle complaints will almost certainly lead to damage to the organisation's reputation. Research shows, on the other hand, that customers whose complaints are handled to their satisfaction are likely to become even more loyal than those who had no complaint to begin with. This is logical. People understand that things go wrong occasionally, but knowing that they are dealing with an organisation that will put things right is reassuring.

Activity 4
Handling complaints

Objective

Use this activity to assess the complaint-handling behaviour in your organisation. The objective of this activity is to identify ways in which the complaint-handling procedures can be used to add value to the corporate reputation. You should also be able to use the activity to consider where improvements might be made in the complaint-handling procedure.

Task

Examine records of complaints made to your organisation in recent months. These may be in the form of letters, e-mails, telephone conversations, letters from lawyers, reports on consumer affairs programmes, or complaints from trade or consumer protection bodies on behalf of customers.

Using the table provided, list the complaints under each category, and record what happened next in terms of complaint handling.

Complainant	Voiced complaint	Third-party complaint	What happened next?

Complainant	Voiced complaint	Third-party complaint	What happened next?

Feedback

It may be that some complaints feature more than once in the list; for example, someone who voiced a complaint but was dissatisfied with the result might well complain again, or bring a third party to bear on the issue.

On the positive side, you may have found that the final column contains occasional feedback from the customer or stakeholder to the effect that the complaint has been handled satisfactorily. The danger signal would be if the complaint had been treated dismissively by the organisation and nothing has been heard from the customer since.

The question here is what can be done about this? You might want to consider ways of improving the feedback from complaining customers to ensure that they are completely happy with the outcome. You might also be able to identify trends in the complaining behaviour – this might also give clues as to what can be done.

Using outside agencies to build corporate image

Outside public relations agencies are frequently used for developing corporate image. The reasons for doing this might be that:

- the organisation is too small to warrant having a specialist PR department

- external agencies have expertise which the organisation lacks

- the external agency can provide an unbiased view of the organisation's needs

- external agencies often carry greater credibility than internal departments or managers

- economies of scale may make the external agency cheaper to use

- one-off events or campaigns can be more efficiently run by outsiders and the organisation's attention is not deflected from its core activities.

What an outside agency might do

The Public Relations Consultants' Association lists the following activities as services that a consultancy might offer:

- establishing channels of communication with the client's public or publics

- management communications

- marketing and sales promotion-related activity

- advice or services relating to political, governmental or public affairs

- financial public relations, dealing with shareholders and investment tipsters

- personnel and industrial relations advice

- recruitment, training, and higher and technical education.

Source: *Public Relations Consultants' Association*

This list is not exhaustive. Since outside agencies often specialise, an organisation may need to go to several different sources to access all the services listed above. Even organisations with an in-house public relations department may prefer to subcontract some specialist or one-off activities. Some activities which may involve an outside agency are:

- **Exhibitions** The infrequency of attendance at exhibitions, for most organisations, means that in-house planning is likely to be disruptive and inefficient. Outside consultants may set up four or five exhibitions a week, compared with the average organisation's four or five a year, so they will have strong expertise in exhibition management.

- **Sponsorship** Outside consultants will have contacts and negotiating expertise which is unlikely to be available in-house. In particular, an outside agency will have up-to-date knowledge of what the 'going rate' is for sponsoring particular events and individuals.

- **Production of house journals** Because of the economies of scale available in the printing and publishing industry, house journals can often be produced more cheaply by outsiders than by the organisation itself.

- **Corporate or financial PR** Corporate PR relies heavily on having a suitable network of contacts in the finance industry and the financial press. It is extremely unlikely that an organisation's PR department will have a comprehensive list of such contacts, so the outside agency provides an instant network of useful contacts.

- **Parliamentary liaison** Lobbying MPs is an extremely specialised area of public relations, requiring considerable insider knowledge and an understanding of current political issues. Professional lobbyists are far better able to carry out this work than an organisation's own public relations officer.

- **Organising one-off events** Like exhibitions, one-off events are almost certainly better subcontracted to an outside agency.

- **Overseas PR** Organisations are extremely unlikely to have the specialist local knowledge necessary for setting up public relations activities in a foreign country.

You can decide which tasks the agency should carry out for you by a process of elimination. Begin by deciding which tasks you are able to carry out in-house, and then whatever tasks are left can be contracted out to the agency – see Figure 2.2.

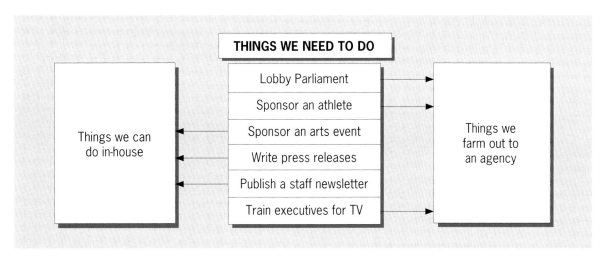

Figure 2.2 *Deciding which tasks to contract out*

Choosing an appropriate agency or consultancy begins with looking at the agency's ability to carry out the specific tasks you need. Table 2.3 shows some of the trade-offs involved in choosing a PR consultancy.

Characteristic	Considerations to be made
Years in business	A long-established consultancy is likely to be experienced and reliable: on the other hand, it may be lacking in new ideas
Size	A large consultancy may have a wide range of services to offer, but may not be interested in a small account
Full service or specialist?	Specialists get very good at one thing: full-service agencies offer a one-stop-shop which helps in co-ordinating activities
Degree of fit with client company	Is the client company local, national or international? Does the agency have experience of other firms in the same business?
Client list	Are there conflicts of interest? Does the consultancy lose a lot of clients? Who are the existing clients?
Staff	How experienced and qualified are the staff who will work on your account? What other accounts will they handle? What is the staff turnover at the consultancy?
Results	Does the consultancy understand what you need? How will results be measured and reported? What will it cost – and on what basis will payment be made?

Table 2.3 *Choosing a PR consultancy*

Unless the outside agency has been called in as a result of a sudden crisis, which is possibly the worst way to handle both PR and consultants, the consultancy will be asked to present a proposal. This allows the consultancy time to research the client's situation and its existing relationships with its publics. The proposal should contain comments on the following aspects of the task:

◆ analysis of the problems and opportunities facing the client organisation

◆ analysis of the potential harm or gain to the client

- analysis of the potential difficulties and opportunities presented by the case, and the various courses of action (or inaction) which would lead to those outcomes
- the overall programme goals and the objectives for each of the target publics
- analysis of any immediate action needed
- long-range planning for achieving the objectives
- monitoring systems for checking the outcomes
- staffing and budgets required for the programme.

Client organisations will often ask several agencies to present, with the aim of choosing the best among them. This approach can cause problems, for several reasons. Firstly, the best agencies may not want to enter into a competitive tendering situation. Secondly, some agencies will send their best people to present, but will actually give the work to their more junior staff. Thirdly, agencies may not want to present their best ideas, feeling (rightly in some cases) that the prospective client will steal their ideas. Finally, it is known that some clients will invite presentations from agencies in order to keep their existing agency on its toes. Such practices are ethically dubious and do no good for the client organisation's reputation. Since the whole purpose of the exercise is to improve the organisation's reputation, annoying the PR agencies is clearly not an intelligent move. To counter the possibility of potential clients stealing their ideas, some of the leading agencies now charge a fee for bidding.

Relationships with external PR consultancies tend to last. Some major organisations have used the same PR consultants for over 20 years. Frequently changing consultants is not a good idea. Consultants need time to build up knowledge of the organisation and its personnel, and the organisation needs time to develop a suitable atmosphere of trust. The consultancy needs to be aware of sensitive information if it is not to be taken by surprise in a crisis, and the client organisation is unlikely to feel comfortable with this unless the relationship has been established for some time.

Developing a brief

The purpose of the brief is to bridge the gap between what the client needs and what the consultant is able to supply. Without a clear brief, the consultant has no blueprint to follow, and neither party has any way of knowing whether the exercise has been successful or not.

Developing a brief begins with the organisation's objectives. Objective setting is a strategic decision area, so it is likely to be the province of senior management. Each objective needs to meet SMARTT criteria:

- ◆ Specific – in other words, it must relate to a narrow range of outcomes
- ◆ Measurable – if it is not measurable, it is merely an aim
- ◆ Achievable – there is no point in setting objectives which cannot be achieved or which are unlikely to be achieved
- ◆ Relevant to the organisation's situation and resources
- ◆ Targeted accurately
- ◆ Timed – a deadline should be in place for its achievement.

The objectives will dictate the budget if the organisation is using the objective-and-task method of budgeting. This method means deciding what tasks need to be undertaken to achieve the final outcome and working out how much it will cost to achieve each task. Most organisations tend to operate on the all-we-can-afford budgeting method, which involves agreeing a figure with the finance director. In these circumstances, the SMARTT formula implies that the budget will dictate the objectives since the objectives must be achievable within the available resources.

Setting the objectives is, of course, only the starting point. Objectives need to be translated into tactical methods for their achievement, and these tactics also need to be considered in the light of what the organisation is trying to achieve.

The brief will be fine-tuned in consultation with the PR agency. From the position of its specialist knowledge, the agency will be able to say whether the budget is adequate for what needs to be achieved or, conversely, say whether the objectives can be achieved within the budget on offer. The agency can also advise on what the appropriate objectives should be, given the organisation's current situation.

Figure 2.3 outlines the process of establishing a brief.

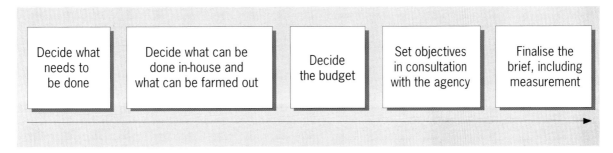

Figure 2.3 *Establishing a brief*

Measuring outcomes

If the outcomes from the PR activities do not match up with the budgeted objectives, conflict between the client and the agency is likely to result. The most common reason for the relationship breaking down is conflict over the costs and hours billed compared with the outcomes achieved. From the agency's viewpoint, much of what happens is outside its direct control. Sponsored events might not attract sufficient audiences, press releases might be spiked as a result of major news stories breaking and special events might be rained off. Many a carefully planned, reputation-enhancing exercise has foundered when the celebrity athlete involved has been caught taking drugs, for example.

Measuring outcomes needs to be considered at the objective-setting stage. A good PR agency will not offer any guarantees of outcomes, but it should be feasible to assign probabilities to the outcomes and to put systems in place for assessing whether the objectives were achieved.

Table 2.4 gives some examples of evaluation methods for PR activities. This list is by no means comprehensive, of course.

Activity	Possible evaluation methods
Press campaign to raise awareness	Formal market research to determine public awareness of the brand/organisation
Campaign to improve the public image	Formal market research: ♦ focus groups for perceptual mapping of the organisation against competitors ♦ measures of attitude change
Exhibition or trade show	Records of contacts made, tracking of leads, formal research to determine improvements in image
Sponsorship of a sporting event	Recall rates for the sponsorship activity

Table 2.4 *PR evaluation methods*

Although market research is a complex topic which is outside the scope of this book, it is possible to identify the stages in the process of measuring PR outcomes. An outline of the approach has been provided by Rossi and Freeman (1999), which is shown in Table 2.5.

Programme conceptualisation and design	What is the extent and distribution of the target problem and/or population?
	Is the programme designed in conformity with intended goals. Is there a coherent rationale underlying it, and have chances of successful delivery been maximised?
	What are project or existing costs, and what is their relation to benefits and effectiveness?
Monitoring and accountability of programme implementation	Is the programme reaching the specified population or target area?
	Are the intervention efforts being conducted as specified in the programme design?
Assessment of programme utility, impact and efficiency	Is the programme effective in achieving its intended goals?
	Can the results of the programme be explained by some alternative process that does not include the programme?
	Is the programme having some effects that were not intended?
	What are the costs to deliver services and benefits to programme participants?
	Is the programme an efficient use of resources compared with alternative uses of the resources?

Table 2.5 *The evaluation research process*   Source: *Rossi and Freeman* (1999)

If these questions are answered in the negative, questions should be asked either about the realism of the objectives or about the tactics the agency has used. If everything goes wrong, it is tempting to fire the agency and try another firm, but in practice this may not be the best answer. Both agency and client will have learned from the experience, possibly at some expense, and it is probably better to stay together and learn the lesson than to split up and have to ride the learning curve all over again with another agency.

Activity 5
Deciding whether to use an agency

Objective

Use this activity to decide whether your organisation should use an agency for some (or all) of its corporate reputation activities. The purpose of the exercise is to assess whether it might be either cheaper or more effective to use an agency rather than carry out the same activities in-house. You might also be able to identify areas in which an agency would be able to carry out a task which is currently not being undertaken at all – in other words, a task which would benefit the organisation but which is currently being ignored for whatever reason.

Task

Using the framework provided below, list the reputation management activities which you believe your organisation is carrying out or should carry out.

In the next column, list the resources necessary to accomplish the task.

In the next column, list the resources which you have available for completing the task.

The final column should contain a list of resources which are needed but which are not available. The question is, should you find a way to provide these resources in-house, or should you farm the activity out to an agency?

Activity	Resources needed	Resources available	Resource shortfall

Feedback

There is almost always a resources shortfall, even for those activities which are already carried out in-house. This makes the decision difficult as to whether it would be more efficient to use an agency.

The decision ultimately rests on whether the expected returns in terms of improved corporate reputation justify the extra outlay (if any) in hiring an agency. This decision in turn rests on whether the outlay will be large or small in relation to the improvements which using an agency will bring.

◆ Recap

Explore how the corporate image adds to stakeholder value

◆ The corporate image should add value to the stakeholders' assets by creating a secure, growing, long-term investment, rather than a short-term gain.

◆ The value that accrues from image management is accounted for as 'goodwill' on the balance sheet. The goodwill element of a company's value is the difference between the value of its tangible assets and its value on the stock market.

Explore the benefits and considerations of sponsorship and word-of-mouth communication as image development techniques

◆ Sponsorship works by transferring the positive feeling that a customer has for the sponsored event to the sponsor organisation. The event or organisation being sponsored should be consistent with the sponsor's brand image and offer a strong possibility of reaching the desired target audience.

◆ People trust word-of-mouth communication, especially from people that they regard as opinion leaders or as knowledgeable about a particular product. However, word-of-mouth communication is difficult to control and can be negative.

◆ Organisations use press releases, bring-a-friend schemes, and awards and certificates to encourage positive word-of-mouth communication.

Identify ways of handling complaints so as to increase customer loyalty

◆ There are three types of complaining behaviour: **voiced response**, **third-party response** and **private response**.

- Redress is usually provided as a replacement product or repeat service, refund or voucher and, in some cases, compensation for consequential losses.

- The key factors influencing how to handle a complaint are the strength of the complaint, the degree of blame attaching to the supplier and the legal and moral relationship between the customer and supplier.

Understand the issues surrounding the appointment and control of outside agencies

- Consultancies and agencies exist for two reasons: firstly, to carry out activities for which the organisation does not have resources, and, secondly, to carry out activities which, because of its specialist expertise, it can do better than the organisation.

- External agencies take time to build up their knowledge of your organisation so be prepared to invest more time at the start of your relationship. Create a brief with SMARTT objectives and put in place an evaluation process to measure whether these have been achieved.

Identify the key factors in choosing an outside agency

- These factors include length of time in the business, size, full service or specialist, degree of fit with your organisation, its client list, calibre of staff and how well it understands the results that you need.

 **More @**

Balmer, J. and Greyser, S. (eds) (2003) *Revealing the Corporation: Perspectives on Identity, Image, Reputation and Corporate Branding*, Routledge
The book draws on articles from leading journals in the field and includes important recent articles as well as classics, written by recognised masters of the genre, which still inform current debate and practice.

Schultz, M., Hatch, M. and Larsen M. H. (2000) *The Expressive Organization: Linking Identity, Reputation and the Corporate Brand*, Oxford University Press
According to the authors, the future lies with 'the expressive organization'. Such organisations not only understand their distinct identity and their brands, but are also able to express these externally and internally.

www.sponsorship.com There are a number of interesting resources at the **IEG Inc.** site, including a good Learn About Sponsorship section, a news section and even job information. Some areas require registration.

Find comprehensive best practice guides on finding an external communications partner and on the construction of a brief at the website for the **Public Relations Consultants' Association**, www.prca.org.uk/sites/prca.nsf/homepages/homepage. These free guides are downloadable.

3 Creating and managing brand image

At the business level, images are largely concerned with branding of products. To an extent, the organisation's image is defined by what it produces, and what it produces is defined by its brand images.

In this theme you will:

◆ Explore what is meant by brand image and how it adds value to an organisation

◆ Identify the elements which go to make up brand image

◆ Evaluate the brand offer of your organisation

◆ Identify ways in which brand communication influences buyer behaviour

◆ Understand how brands operate as communication devices.

Branding

Because many products are similar to each other, people often do not particularly care which one they buy; for example, there is very little functional difference between brands of petrol, whether it is sold by Shell, Esso, BP or Elf. Products like this are called commodity products because they are homogeneous commodities which do not offer different benefits from other products in the same category. The purpose of branding is to differentiate the organisation's products and create a source of competitive advantage by making the product stand out from the crowd.

> Suppliers and especially manufacturers have market power because they have information about a product or a service that the customer does not and cannot have, and does not need if he can trust the brand. This explains the profitability of brands.
>
> **Peter Drucker**
> **Business author and strategist**

Commodity products versus branded products

Commodity products are those which are very similar from the customer's viewpoint and which are usually bought on the basis of price. This means that profit margins are likely to be small unless the producer has a strong cost advantage. For this reason, producers try to avoid their products becoming commodities and try to differentiate their product from the others on the market. For example, drinking water is an example of a commodity product, yet supermarkets stock a range of bottled waters, each with its own formulation and brand name, and each appealing to a different group of consumers who do not regard the product as a commodity at all. In these cases, the original commodity product has been converted into a brand. Branding is a process of adding value to the product by the use of packaging, name, promotion, and position in the minds of the consumers.

De Chernatony and McDonald (2003) offer the following definition of brand:

> A successful brand is an identifiable product, service, person or place, augmented in such a way that the buyer or user perceives relevant, unique added values which match their needs most closely. Furthermore, its success results from being able to sustain those added values in the face of competition.

Most of us recognise the value of buying a familiar brand rather than a generic or commodity product. The consumer value that is added includes reassurance of the brand's quality, the status that may accrue from using that brand (because the brand's image carries over to the consumer) and convenience of purchase (because the brand is easy to recognise on the supermarket shelf). The same considerations apply in business-to-business markets. For example, a parcel delivery company will choose vehicles which have a good brand reputation since this reflects on the quality of its own brand.

Figure 3.1 shows the relationship between commodity products and branded products in terms of image and price.

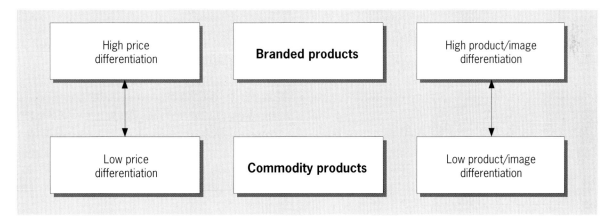

Figure 3.1 *Commodity products versus branded products*

Because commodity products such as petrol are usually undifferentiated in price, a differential of even 10 per cent would be very noticeable. By definition, they also have a low degree of differentiation in product characteristics and image. Branded goods, on the other hand, score high on both factors; since they command a premium price, they show more profit per unit. The cost of establishing and maintaining the brand needs to be deducted from this, but there is still value in trying to establish a strong brand.

Strategic issues in branding

Adding value to the product by branding involves a great deal more than merely giving the product a catchy name. Branding involves the whole marketing mix, and the brand is therefore a combination of the price, the product itself, the place from which it is available and the promotion used to inform consumers about it. This leads to a brand image, which is a shorthand way of conveying a set of messages about the product to the consumer and, perhaps more importantly, to the consumer's friends and family. The brand lets the consumer know what to expect in terms of quality, price, expected performance and status. For example, the Mercedes brand carries a higher status than some other brands and therefore conveys information about the driver. The same is true of the Mercedes truck brand, which conveys information about the company that operates such vehicles.

Branding is more than simply a tactical tool designed to differentiate the product on the supermarket shelves or in the trade press. It involves all the elements of the marketing mix, so it must be regarded as the focus for the marketing effort as a way of directing management thought and co-ordinating the activities of the organisation towards producing consumer satisfaction. The brand acts as a common point of contact between the producer and the customer, as shown in Figure 3.2.

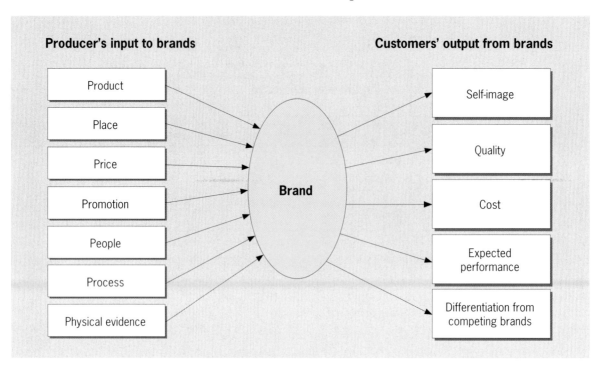

Figure 3.2 *Brands as a contact point*

The brand enables the organisation to stay on track, but it also enables the customers to know what they are going to get from the product. In many cases, the benefit to the customer from owning the product is intangible – in other words, the brand conveys an image that the customer would like to be associated with. This is not necessarily an up-market image; some people take pride in being frugal and getting a bargain, and some organisations like to convey an image of being cost-conscious.

Although many of the benefits are intangible, this does not mean that they are not real. Medical experiments show that branded painkillers work better than generic painkillers, even though the chemical formula is identical; this is because of the psychosomatic power of the brand. Likewise, a teenager wearing the right kind of trainers gains very real benefits in terms of the respect of others, even if the trainers do not perform any better than their cheaper rivals.

Branding has eight different strategic functions, as shown in Figure 3.3.

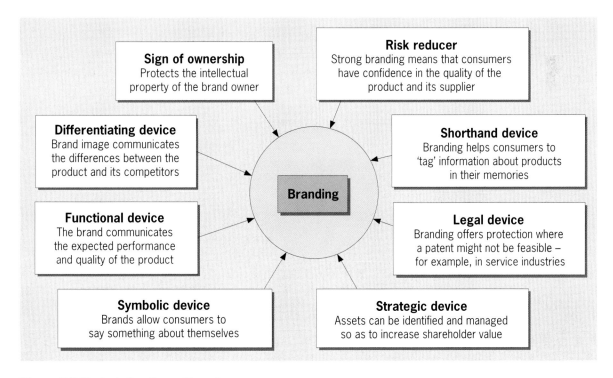

Figure 3.3 *Strategic functions of brands*

Research shows that brands which are held in high esteem tend to be more consistent in their sales, being less likely to suffer when markets turn down (Png and Reitman, 1995). Not all brands are premium brands, of course. Some brands are priced at the lower end of the scale as value-for-money brands, which often means that they have more consistent sales than unbranded goods.

Brands exist as a means of communicating values.

A strong brand means that the organisation does not need to compete on price. This is a valuable consideration, since price competition inevitably cuts profits and there will always be someone who is prepared to take a loss on sales, either through incompetence or through a desire to do business.

Activity 6
Assessing brand values

Objective

Use this activity to assess the brands your organisation offers. The purpose of the activity is to enable you to understand how branding works within your organisation, and what the branding structure is. This should allow you to assess the degree of fit and consistency between the brand values involved.

Task

The diagram provided below has two continuous dimensions: the high price/low price dimension, and the high differentiation/low differentiation dimension. On each dimension, mark the position of each of your organisation's brands and your competitors' brands. This means that each brand will appear twice, once on the left-hand continuum and once on the right-hand continuum.

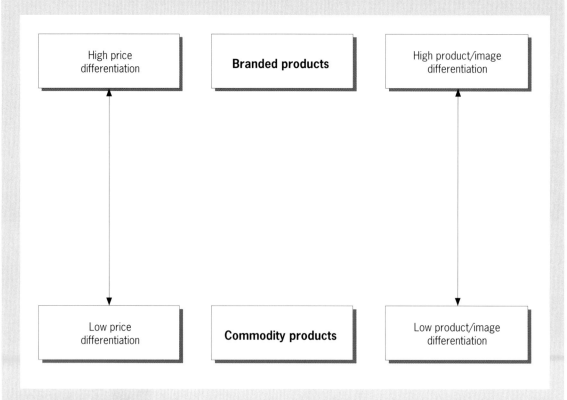

It is probable that some brands will occupy a higher position on one continuum than they do on the other. What does this imply about the performance of that brand in the market? What could be done about it, in a practical sense?

Implication for performance and solution:

Feedback

It is almost certain that some of the brands you identified will occupy different relative positions on each continuum. The reason for this is that the position on the continuum is not an absolute – it depends heavily on your personal view of the brand values, and especially your perception of value for money.

The implication of having a brand which is high in price but not very differentiated in product and image is that the product will seem like exceptionally bad value for money. A product low in price and highly differentiated might appear to be exceptionally good value; a product low in price and low in differentiation will seem to be priced correctly, as will a highly differentiated product which is also high in price.

You may want to try the same experiment with a colleague or friend to see if the perception is the same for both of you. Although this is a simplistic, two-dimensional assessment, it does show that people differ in their assessments of brands and that brands may not always be priced correctly, at least in the opinion of a given individual.

You may also wish to consider what the consequences are of this type of discrepancy. In some cases the discrepancy is small, so the effects will also be small, but in other cases the effects might be considerable, either on sales or on profits.

Branding and buyer behaviour

Ultimately, branding can only be effective in terms of its effect on the organisation's customers. Brands have a role to play in the behaviour of buyers and this should not be underestimated.

Brands and positioning

The simpler it is for people to buy a product, the more likely it is that purchases will result. Because most purchases are routine, branding is a useful device for reducing decision-making time and the effort of evaluating competing products. The human brain stores information as a series of 'chunks', triggered by key words or symbols. Branding provides appropriate keys to access the information so that customers are able to recall an overall impression of the brand efficiently.

In most cases, people store information on several brands within the product category and are able to access this information in order to make comparisons between brands. In order to establish a brand in people's minds, marketers need to promote effectively, but more importantly they need to ensure that the product and everything that surrounds it corresponds to the brand image being conveyed.

Placing the brand in the right place in the customer's perceptual map relative to other brands is called positioning. Individuals decide where the product belongs in relation to other products on the basis of what they expect and believe to be the product's attributes. Information for making this decision comes from three main sources: advertising, word-of-mouth communications and direct experience. For a brand to be successfully positioned, all three of these must deliver much the same message, or cognitive dissonance will occur – see Figure 3.4. Cognitive dissonance is a state of affairs whereby the individual has to reconcile conflicting information.

In Figure 3.4, Brand A's managers have ensured that the advertising, word of mouth and actual experiences of the customer are telling the same story so that the product is correctly positioned. Brand X's managers, on the other hand, have not co-ordinated the factors, and therefore the product has no clear position in the customer's perceptual map. Each element is giving a different message about where the product belongs so that confusion results for the customer. This will lead in turn to feelings of uncertainty, which increases the perceived risk of buying the product.

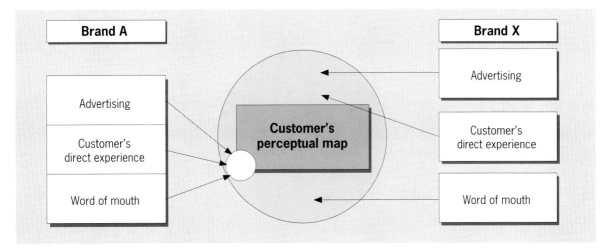

Figure 3.4 *Co-ordinated and unco-ordinated messages*

The first stage in positioning is to determine what the pertinent features of the product category are from the customers' viewpoint. This gives the basis on which the product will be judged. The marketer can then adjust the mix of product features and benefits to gain competitive advantage with one or other of the target groups in the market.

Product positioning will depend on the existing attitudes of customers within the target market. Marketers can either accept these attitudes as they are and tailor the product offering around them, or they can seek to change the existing attitudes. It is almost always cheaper and easier to change the product than it is to change the attitudes of customers, but sometimes the attitudes of customers are so negative that there is no choice but to embark on a re-education programme.

Activity 7
Branding and attitudes

Objective

Use this activity to assess the integration of your organisation's branding messages. The objective of this activity is to highlight areas in which the brand values are not being communicated in a consistent manner to all the organisation's publics. The exercise will also help you to consider ways in which the brand values might be communicated more effectively.

Task

Obtain copies of your organisation's communications materials. This will include such items as advertising, press releases, shareholder reports, letterheads and even letters to customers. Considering the brand values of the organisation, assess the degree to which the communications reflect the brand values.

In cases where there is a discrepancy, what might you do to correct the imbalance?

Assessment of degree to which communications reflect brand values and suggestions for correcting any imbalance:

Feedback

Almost certainly you will find some discrepancies between what you think of as the organisation's brand values and the values contained in the corporate communications. This may be because you have a different view of the organisation's brand values from that of the producers of the materials, but it is more likely that there are real discrepancies in the materials, especially if the material concerned is a customer letter.

This is a problem for brand managers since so many people are involved in producing corporate communications. There are several possible solutions. One is to insist that all external communications are vetted by the brand managers or PR people. In practice, this is almost impossible to do because it creates an unacceptable workload. A more practical approach is to establish the corporate and brand values strongly in the minds of the members of the organisation. This will help to ensure that each member communicates the same values whatever the circumstances.

This aspect of internal marketing is basic to integrating the brand values.

Brands as communications

Brands exist as a means of communicating values about the product to the consumers.

Brand names

A brand name is a term, symbol or design that distinguishes one seller's product from its competitors. It is not the brand itself; it is just the identifying symbols for it which enable consumers to recognise the brand and deduce at least some of its characteristics. There are several factors to be taken into account when formulating brand names:

1 **Marketing objectives** The brand name must fit the marketing objectives of the organisation and these must fit the organisation's corporate objectives. For example, a company that has developed brands aimed at children will need brand names that appeal to a young audience.

2 **Brand audit** This is a critical examination of the various factors that impinge on the brand and its values, including internal factors and external factors such as competitive actions.

3 **Brand objectives** This is a breakdown of the corporate and marketing objectives according to individual brands. Each brand should contribute to the overall objectives of the organisation. For example, companies which intend to cover a wide range of markets will need to have specific branding for each market or market segment.

4 **Brand strategy alternatives** Almost certainly there will be other ways of achieving the brand's objectives. These may need to be taken into consideration when choosing a name.

Brand names can be protected by registration in most countries, but UK law provides some protection for unregistered brands in that it is illegal to try to 'pass off' one product for another. For example, using a similar brand name to that of a famous brand or even using a similar package design could be regarded as 'passing off'. This is a civil offence, not a criminal one, so it is up to the offended brand owner to take legal action. McDonald's restaurants have for some time been trying to prevent UK fast-food restaurants (and even other companies not in the fast-food business) from using the 'Mc' prefix. The success of such actions has been low, if only because a large number of British surnames have the 'Mc' prefix and it is a general principle of UK law that individuals cannot be prevented from trading under their own name. The result would be entirely different if an organisation tried to use the golden arches symbol, however.

Ries (1995) suggests that brand names should have the following characteristics:

- ◆ They should shock, that is, catch the customer's attention
- ◆ They should be alliterative; this helps them to be memorable
- ◆ They should connect to the product's positioning in the consumer's perceptual map
- ◆ They should link to a visual image; again, this helps the memory
- ◆ They should communicate something about the product, or be capable of being used to communicate about the product
- ◆ They should encourage the development of a nickname – for example Bud for Budweiser beer
- ◆ They should be telephone- and directory-friendly.

Naming a brand is probably as difficult and as important as naming a baby. The brand, like the baby, will carry the name for the rest of its life, so you need to take into account that some words have entirely different meanings in different languages and ensure that the brand is transferable across national and cultural boundaries. Examples of brand names which have failed to do this are legion; Bum crisps and Revoltosa lemonade are popular in Spain, but are unlikely to catch on in the UK, for example.

Brands and semiotics

Semiotics is the study of signs and their meanings. Brands have four levels in terms of semiotics, as shown in Figure 3.5.

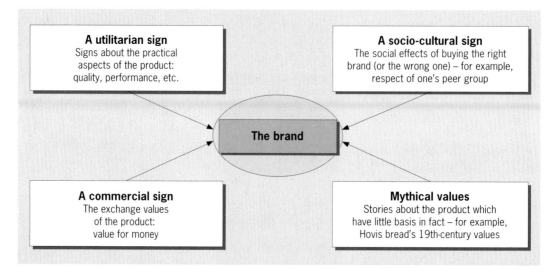

Figure 3.5 *Levels of signs in brands*

Brands do not create myths; they merely build on what is already in place. Mythology provides the conceptual framework within which the daily problems of life can be fitted and from which solutions can be found. Many major brands have mythical connotations. Myths grew up around the Rolls-Royce car regarding its exceptional reliability, and some urban myths address the attributes of brands.

There is a story that a Rolls-Royce owner suffered a breakdown while travelling in a remote area. He called a local garage, which in turn called out the Rolls-Royce engineer, who replaced the broken part. The motorist was duly grateful, but was surprised not to be given a bill for the repair, so he wrote to the company to ask how much he owed. In due course he received this reply: 'We are grateful to have received your letter, but feel there must be some mistake as Rolls-Royce cars do not break down.' No bill was ever sent.

This story was told frequently in the 1950s, even by Rolls-Royce employees, but appears to have no basis in fact.

Marlboro cigarettes play on the Wild West myth of the wide-open spaces in order to give a 'macho' image to the cigarettes. This is interesting, since the Marlboro brand was originally conceived as a cigarette for women, and they were originally available in a range of colours so that women could co-ordinate their cigarettes with their make-up.

Gordon and Valentine (1996) carried out research that showed that different types of retail outlet conveyed different meanings to consumers. Convenience stores conveyed an image of disorder and clutter, coupled with feelings of guilt and confusion that probably relate to having forgotten to buy something. Supermarkets conveyed an image of efficient domestic organisation and planning, and also of functionality. Off-licences legitimated the purchase of alcohol, allowing people to feel comfortable about buying alcohol without the feeling that other shoppers might disapprove. This study is interesting in that it demonstrates that the location where the purchase takes place is also important in decision making. Purchase behaviour is far from being rational, and contains much which is based on emotion.

Brand extensions

A brand extension is another product in the organisation's range which uses a variation on the original brand name. For example, easyJet now operates easyHire car hire services and easyMoney financial services.

The object of the exercise is to cash in on an existing brand name by selling other products with similar brand values under the same umbrella name. Because establishing a brand is a long-term, expensive exercise, organisations may try to maximise the return on the investment by stretching the brand over a range of products. Unfortunately, relatively few brands can be extended indefinitely, and there is a very real risk of damaging the original brand's image. Virgin appeared to be the exception to this rule, having extended the brand from record producing, through retailing, to airlines and financial services, but the attempt to extend the brand to railway trains has proved seriously problematic, with some damage done to the overall brand image.

In the past 10 years, organisations have been grouping products under a common brand to create a composite value greater than that of the components. This is called compositioning. An example would be Disney's practice of designating 'official airlines' and 'official ferry companies' to transport customers to its theme parks. Brand architecture is the way in which brands and sub-brands relate to each other strategically. In the case of compositioning, brand architecture decisions might involve products that are the property of other organisations.

Extending brands across national boundaries is fraught with difficulties, but is obviously necessary if the brand is to continue to grow. Some brands are globalised, with the organisation offering a standard product and often a standardised promotional package as well (for example Coca-Cola) whereas other brands are adapted for each market (as is the case with Heinz). In fact, few companies offer an entirely globalised package. Research shows that only a tiny minority of companies use the same promotional package in all their markets, which means that the brand itself differs in each market. Because brand image is a construct of the producer's marketing mix coupled with the consumer's pre-existing knowledge and prejudices, the brand image will differ in each country anyway. For example, Aldi's retail stores are regarded as good-quality wholesale outlets in its native Germany, but in the UK it is regarded as a low-quality discount retailer.

Activity 8
Communicating the brand

Objective

Use this activity to assess whether your brand's values are communicated effectively to others. The purpose of this exercise is to identify problems in communicating the brand values correctly and effectively by finding out what other people's perceptions of the brand are. This should help you consider ways of improving the communication of brand values and perhaps of changing people's perceptions of the brand.

Task

Use the table provided below to check the brand perceptions of your colleagues or friends. You can use either one of your own organisation's brands or a well-known consumer brand. All respondents should, of course, comment on the same brand!

Write the answers in each box, then check for common responses.

Respondent	If this brand were an animal, what kind of animal would it be?	If this brand were a colour, what colour would it be?	If this brand were a style of music, what style would it be?

Feedback

This exercise usually shows that there is some commonality between the responses people give. The closer the commonality, the better targeted is the branding activity. Therefore, if your respondents all thought the brand was most like a cat, this means that the brand value has come across well. Obviously one would need to refine the research to be sure what people mean by 'cat'. Sometimes the answers given by people within the organisation differ from those given by outsiders because they are looking at the problem from different angles.

Perhaps the most interesting aspect of this exercise is that it is possible at all. People seem to have little difficulty in thinking of a brand in terms of musical styles or colours. This says something about the workings of the human brain.

◆ Recap

Explore what is meant by brand image and how it adds value to an organisation

◆ Branding is the process of adding value to a product or service through, for example, packaging or promotion in order to position its unique attributes in the minds of target consumers and to differentiate it from its competitors.

◆ The main purpose of branding is to improve profitability by charging a premium price and/or increasing customer demand.

Identify the elements which go to make up brand image

◆ Branding is a strategic activity that involves co-ordinating activities and messages across all elements of the marketing mix: product, place, price, promotion, people, process and physical evidence.

◆ A brand that is high in price but is not differentiated in terms of the other elements of the marketing mix will seem like bad value for money.

Evaluate the brand offer of your organisation

◆ Most organisations have more than one product and more than one brand. Organisations typically have an umbrella brand that covers the entire range of products (similar to Ford), and individually branded products that occupy different market niches (Ford Transit versus Ford Ka).

◆ Some organisations offer commodity products that are undifferentiated within their marketplace. These products can be profitable, sometimes even more profitable than competing branded goods, because they do not carry the cost of developing brand image.

Identify ways in which brand communication influences buyer behaviour

◆ A key purpose of branding is to provide consumers with information that will enable them to compare brands and make decisions. The information comes from three main sources: advertising, word-of-mouth communication and direct experience.

◆ Brand managers try to ensure that the brand values are communicated in a consistent way by each of these sources so that the brand occupies a clear position in the consumer's perceptual map. This is called positioning.

Understand how brands operate as communication devices

◆ A brand name should catch the customer's attention, be easy to remember, be consistent with other aspects of product positioning, link to a visual image, communicate something about the product, encourage the development of a nickname and be directory friendly.

◆ A brand consists of more than just a name. A set of values surrounds the brand that convey social, practical, commercial and even mythical concepts about it.

 **More @**

De Chernatony, L. and McDonald, M. (2003) 3rd edition, *Creating powerful brands*, Butterworth-Heinemann
This is one of world's most respected and successful books on branding.

De Chernatony, L. (2003) *From Brand Vision to Brand Value*, Butterworth-Heinemann
Presents the reader with practical applications for brand building that build upon the theoretical background outlined in *Creating powerful brands*.

The **American Marketing Association** provides wide-ranging articles, webcasts and white papers on all aspects of marketing communications, including branding. Registration is free at www.marketingpower.com.

www.knowthis.com is another online portal, the **Marketing Virtual Library**, with a rich source of articles. For the section on branding, try www.knowthis.com/management/branding

4 Managing the internal image

Much of the popular focus on marketing concerns what happens outside the organisation. In fact, it is often what happens within the organisation that has most effect on the corporate image and reputation. Employees go home after work and mix with their families and friends. Their word of mouth carries a great deal more weight than any corporate advertising, and yet employees frequently find it hard to say anything positive about their employers.

In fact work is about much more than merely coming home with a pay cheque. Many people base their identities on their work roles and fulfil social needs through their work. Others meet intellectual needs or find work challenging and interesting. Still others have ambitions that can only be met through being part of an organisation. For these people, a job which pays well but does not meet their other needs is entirely inadequate, and they are likely to seek employment elsewhere.

This theme is about how you can establish a good corporate image among employees, and how you can use public relations and internal marketing to create a corporate culture and manage change within an organisation. The advantages of doing this are that morale tends to rise, staff turnover tends to fall and efficiency tends to improve, but in exchange for this some effort needs to be made and there are costs attached.

In this theme you will:

◆ **Consider why it is important to manage the internal image**

◆ **Explore techniques for managing the internal image**

◆ **Assess the role effectiveness of the house journal in your organisation**

◆ **Consider how internal marketing can be used to support the change process in organisations.**

Internal versus external marketing

Internal marketing and external marketing have some notable differences, as shown in Table 4.1.

Internal marketing	External marketing
Focuses primarily on production of goods and services	Focuses primarily on consumption of goods and services
Uses media which are only available to a small group	Uses publicly available media
Usually directs effort towards individuals whose identities are known in detail	Usually directs effort towards individuals whose identities are unknown
Seeks to generate more profit by reducing costs	Seeks to generate more profit by increasing revenues or profit margin per unit
Seeks to increase shareholder value by improving employee values	Seeks to increase shareholder value by improving brand values
Improves the organisation's survival chances by retaining and nurturing top-grade employees	Improves the organisation's survival chances by improving competitive position

Table 4.1 *Internal versus external marketing*

Since marketing is concerned with the management of exchanges, it seems sensible to assume that internal marketing is about the management of internal exchanges – exchanges that happen within the organisation. These exchanges are numerous and may also be hierarchical. A possible hierarchy is as follows:

◆ exchange of time for salary

◆ exchange of loyalty for supportive management

◆ exchange of effort for respect

◆ exchange of commitment and ideas for information about the organisation's future direction.

Unlike most external marketing, the exchanges cannot always be expressly stated. While the exchange of time for salary (the basic exchange in all employment contracts) is expressly stated and is quantifiable, the other exchanges are harder to define. Having said that, the problem can still be analysed and ultimately solved.

In some cases, the exchange of money for time might be as far as either party wishes to take the relationship. This situation will only arise where employees perform low-grade manual tasks and have little contact with the organisation's customers. In all other cases, employee motivation and attitudes have considerable impact on the success of the organisation. Employees are important in two ways: firstly as stakeholders in the organisation, which means that their motivation and commitment is necessary for the organisation's success; and secondly as ambassadors for the organisation.

Creating pride in the organisation and in its work can be achieved by carrying out the tasks shown in Table 4.2. These factors were identified as a result of research carried out by Kanter (1985) over a five-year period.

Task	Rationale and methods of achievement
Encourage an atmosphere of pride	Highlight the achievements of individuals, publicising these to others. Use innovative staff as agents of change
Provide suitable vehicles for innovation	Have communication channels that allow innovative ideas to be disseminated and acted on across organisational boundaries
Improve lateral communication	This will improve the flow of innovative ideas. Encouraging joint project teams and interdepartmental social events, and exchanging people between departments, where possible, can facilitate this
Cut down layers of hierarchy	By devolving decision making down the hierarchy and by cutting out layers of management, employees can feel more in control of what is happening within the organisation
Increase the available information regarding organisational plans and projects	Reducing secrecy will ensure closer involvement of those who have to implement the plans, and may also lead to a reduction in mistakes caused through unrealistic planning – ground-floor staff are usually much closer to the problem than senior management
Ensure that the leadership is aware of its limited perspective	Running the organisation from the top is unlikely to be as effective as giving employees more control over events, provided of course that the employees are attuned to the organisation's objectives

Table 4.2 *Tasks for improving staff perception of the organisation*

Source: *Adapted from Kanter* (1985)

From the employee's perspective, the organisation needs to supply answers to these questions (D'Apris, 1987):

1 What's my job?

2 How am I doing?

3 Does anybody give a damn?

Once the organisation has answered these questions, the employee will want answers to these:

4 How are we doing?

5 How do we fit in to the whole?

6 How can I help?

The last of these questions is, of course, the one that the management of the organisation is most ready to answer. The task of answering all these questions is part of the remit of the internal PR systems of the organisation. The public relations people sometimes generate the tools used for this, though more often the personnel department of the organisation carries out the task. Typical internal PR tools are:

♦ corporate intranets

♦ internal newsletters

♦ staff magazines

♦ staff meetings.

Rowntree Mackintosh

Rowntree Mackintosh takes internal communications seriously. The company has a history of employee involvement going back to the days of its Quaker founders, but during the 1970s and 1980s management established a comprehensive employee communications system.

Within the company there is a team-briefing process that involves all employees in problem solving. The teams find solutions to problems within their own departments and pass these on to management for implementation. The company newspaper appears in five local editions each month, and employees each get an annual report of their own, in addition to the shareholders' annual report. Twice a year employees are given a comprehensive briefing on the state of the business, and there is a profit-sharing scheme and quality circles that meet regularly to maintain (and improve on) standards. At every level and for every problem there is employee involvement – and it pays off.

Senior management report that this high level of involvement and trust has led to a greater level of understanding among the employees. This in turn has generated lower absenteeism and greater productivity, but this is the least of the results. Most importantly of all, it is virtually impossible to find a Rowntree Mackintosh employee who has a bad word to say about the company – and that is a rare thing in this day and age!

The Rowntree Mackintosh example shows that there is more to good employee relations than merely maintaining the company noticeboard and writing a newsletter. Real commitment of management to employee involvement is essential and has to go beyond mere communication of management decisions.

Activity 9
Managing the internal image

Objective

Use this activity to examine the internal image of the organisation. The purpose of the exercise is to identify the positive and negative aspects of the organisation from the employee's viewpoint, in particular looking at some of the key characteristics which employees regard as fundamental to their jobs. This should enable you to consider ways of improving the internal image and of improving morale by maintaining the positive aspects and minimising the negative aspects of the organisation's image.

Task

Ask a selection of colleagues to rate the organisation on the attributes shown in the table provided. Ask them to assign a score out of 10, with 10 as the highest rating.

Salary: fair pay	Supportive management	Respect in the workplace	Information about the organisation's future

What is the average score for the organisation on each attribute?

What might be the effects of scoring low on each one?

What might be the effects of scoring high?

Feedback

Sometimes people are more negative in their statements than they need to be. This is because it is sometimes part of the organisational culture to be negative: employees who refer to their employer as 'this place' are often making a political statement rather than expressing a true feeling.

Having said that, a consistently low score on one or other of the attributes will lead one to suspect that there is a problem. If the employer is offering an unattractive exchange, or offering little in exchange, the employees might feel entitled to reduce what they offer.

Low salaries mean a lowered propensity to continue the exchange. This might manifest itself as a higher staff turnover, as an increase in absenteeism or as a 'we pretend to work and they pretend to pay us' attitude.

Unsupportive management discourages loyalty. Loyalty works both ways, and staff who do not feel supported will seeks ways of protecting themselves rather than concentrating on the job in hand.

Respect is basic to human relationships. Although respect should be earned, it is advisable to begin by showing respect, even if this later turns out to be misplaced. Employees who do not feel respected are unlikely to make much effort.

Information about the organisation's future encourages employees to become involved in the process. This in turn encourages ideas and improves commitment to the long-term aims of the organisation.

Of course, these exchanges are tacit rather than overt: managers do not say 'If you do this, I will do that' as a regular way of managing staff. Nevertheless, the days when managers could simply tell staff what to do and expect automatic obedience are long gone.

The role of public relations in the organisation

Public relations is often seen as an external activity forming the opinions of outsiders. In fact, it has a crucial role to play in developing the corporate culture.

Reading this article will help you to:

◆ understand how PR activities can improve staff morale and retention

◆ explore ways of improving internal PR

◆ develop techniques for guiding the corporate culture.

Organisational needs

Organisations, just like people, have needs. Some of these needs are common to all organisations, and have different levels of importance according to the circumstances of the organisation or the particular stage in its development. A hierarchy of organisational needs was developed by Pearson (1980). Table 4.3 shows how PR can help in satisfying those needs.

Organisational need	Requirements	Typical PR activity
Output	Money, machines, manpower, materials	Staff programmes to attract the right people
Survival	Cash flow, profits, share performance, customers	Publicity aimed at customers. Events publicising the organisation and its products
Morale	Employee job satisfaction	Staff newsletters, morale-boosting activities, etc.
Acceptability	Approval by the external stakeholders – shareholders, government, customers, suppliers, society in general	External PR, shareholder reports, lobbying of government departments and MPs, events for suppliers and customers, favourable press releases
Leadership	Having a respected position in the organisation's chosen field – this could be due to customer satisfaction, employee involvement, industry leadership in technology, or several of these	Corporate image-building exercises, customer care activities, publicity about new products and technological advances, sponsorship of research in universities, sponsorship of the arts

Table 4.3 *The hierarchy of organisational needs*

Pearson's hierarchy is useful as a concept but less useful as a practical guide because so many organisations vary the order in which these needs are met.

Sony Corporation

When Akio Morita (and others) founded the Sony Corporation just after the Second World War the directors decided that corporate unity and staff involvement in the running of the company were paramount.

At the time, due to post-war shortages, the company was having difficulty getting materials to work with and a factory from which to operate. Employees were relatively easy to find – the Japanese Army was gradually returning home, and many qualified electronics engineers were available. However, their morale was low, and often their physical condition and their personal lives were not in good shape. Morita (an ex-Navy engineer himself) arranged for the employees to have a company uniform so that the distinction between management and staff would be less obvious, and also to give the outside world a good impression of the company. There was also a less high-flown aspect to this apparently enlightened approach – many of the employees had only ragged clothes or the remnants of their army uniforms, so Morita was able to ensure loyalty because so many of his staff literally had nothing to wear other than the company uniform.

Sony employees felt confident that they were working with, rather than for, the corporation and co-operated wholeheartedly in getting the fledgling company off the ground. Other Japanese companies followed a similar approach to that of Sony, with a long-lasting effect on the culture of Japan. Staff turnover in Japan is a tiny fraction of what it is in Western countries, and companies such as Sony enjoy a worldwide reputation for good business ethics.

Source: *Based on Morita* (1987)

Internal communications media

House journal

House journals are printed information books or sheets that are made available to employees. Journals may be of any of the following types:

♦ **Magazine** Containing feature articles and illustrations, magazines are relatively expensive to produce but have a professional, credible feel about them.

♦ **Newspaper** These can be produced to resemble a tabloid newspaper, which makes them more accessible to some groups of employees. The contents consist of news articles about the organisation, with some feature articles.

♦ **Newsletter** Common in small organisations, a newsletter will probably be A4 or foolscap size, and will contain brief items, usually without illustration. Newsletters are cheap and easy to produce, especially in small numbers.

♦ **Wall newspaper** These look like posters and are displayed on walls. They are useful for brief communications about events or changes in organisational policies.

♦ **Electronic newsletter** Internal e-mail systems offer great potential for disseminating newsletters. The medium is cheap to use, effective, and often increases the likelihood that the newsletter will be read. Furthermore, it is possible to tell who opened the newsletter and who deleted it without reading it – although, of course, opening it is not the same as reading it.

When planning a house journal, you need to consider the issues shown in Figure 4.1:

♦ **Readership** Different groups of staff may have different needs, so it may be necessary to produce different journals for each. Research workers are likely to have different needs from truck drivers, for instance.

♦ **Quality** The greater the number of copies, the lower the production cost per copy. If the number of employees is large, a better-quality journal can be produced; if the number is small, the organisation may need to produce newsletters or wall newspapers instead.

♦ **Frequency** Frequent publication means that the journal is more likely to become part of the daily routine of staff. Some large organisations even publish such journals daily.

◆ **Policy** The journal should be more than simply a propaganda device for senior management. It should fit in with an overall PR programme and should have a clear editorial policy to ensure the quality of its content.

◆ **Title** The title should be characteristic of the organisation. Changing the title is difficult once it has become established, as with any brand name.

◆ **Printing process** To an extent the printing process will affect the content, since simple, cheap printing processes cannot reproduce some illustrations. Cost will also affect the choice of process, as will the desire for a good-quality, credible journal.

◆ **Style and format** Credibility is linked to the degree to which the journal resembles a commercial magazine. Style and format are part of the communication in the same way that packaging is part of a product.

◆ **Price** Obviously the vast majority of house journals are free to staff, but it is feasible to make a charge if the journal is sufficiently interesting. There is no reason why a cover price should not be put on the journal in any case, even if it is free. This conveys to the staff that the journal is valuable and thus it is more likely to be read.

◆ **Advertisements** Carrying advertising may be a useful way to reduce costs. If the circulation is sufficiently large, outside organisations might be prepared to place advertising – this is particularly true if the producer of the journal is a large organisation operating from a single location, since local shops, restaurants and entertainment venues might well wish to promote their products. Employees may well want to advertise items for sale or forthcoming social events and this also increases the readability of the journal.

◆ **Distribution** Journals can be delivered by hand, by post to the employee's home address or from distribution points within the organisation (such as mail pigeonholes). The decision will be based on the frequency of publication, the location of employees and the type of journal involved. Distribution via e-mail is probably the quickest and cheapest method.

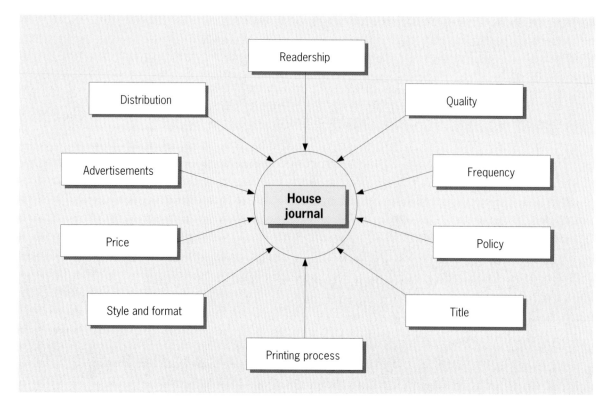

Figure 4.1 *Issues to consider in designing a house journal*

House journals are often edited independently of senior management to ensure that the focus is on the employees' need for information rather than on the management's need to control or manipulate.

Websites

Many organisations now operate internal websites or intranets – aimed at employees. These sites cannot be accessed by outsiders and they fulfil the same function as the house journal. The main advantage is that the costs are greatly reduced compared with producing a house journal. The disadvantage is that employees are unlikely to access the site except during working hours and in some cases may not be able to access the site at all because the nature of their work does not involve using a computer.

Internal websites are most useful in organisations in which virtually every employees is provided with a computer and in which there is no problem about allowing employees to scan the website during working hours. Website design is a specialist area, but some rules have been developed: sites need to be simple to access and use; graphics should be kept simple to minimise download time; and, as far as possible, articles should fit onto one screen.

Internal briefings and open meetings

Some organisations give staff the opportunity to have access to senior management at open meetings or briefings. These briefings have the advantage of allowing senior management to gain direct access to grass-roots views from the workforce, as well as giving the workforce the chance to question senior managers about organisational policies.

The overall effect is to increase openness within the organisation and break down barriers. In general, employees work better if they understand why things are being done the way they are being done. This understanding also enables them to use their initiative better if the system breaks down for any reason.

Activity 10
House journals

Objective

Use this activity to assess your house journal. The objective here is to enable you to identify ways in which the journal might be improved, and in particular to help you identify ways in which the internal marketing of the organisation could be helped by better design of the house journal.

Task

Using the list of issues in Figure 4.1, analyse the house journal of your organisation. If your organisation does not have a house journal, you might be able to obtain one from a friend who works for a different organisation.

Use the table provided for your analysis.

Readership	Printing process
Quality	Style and format
Frequency	Price
Policy	Advertisements
Title	Distribution

What changes would you make to the factors you have identified in order to improve the effectiveness of the journal? What results would you hope to obtain from these changes?

Do you think your colleagues would make different changes?

Changes	Results from change	Colleagues' changes?

Feedback

Obviously the changes you might want to make are somewhat subjective, but in many cases the essential problem with a house journal lies in ensuring that the employees actually read it.

For this reason, you will probably have focused on the policy, distribution, style and format. You might expect an increase in readership to follow on from making changes in these areas.

Internal marketing and change management

During the 1990s and the early part of the 21st century, change management has been one of the main preoccupations of management thinking. This is due to a perception that we are living in times of rapid change, and therefore the ability to change the organisation in order to adapt to environmental changes is essential for survival. Whether or not this is true remains to be seen, but there is no doubt that change is unpopular among employees. Most people are suspicious of change, particularly when something as fundamental as their working life is involved, and a typical response to any proposed change is likely to be one of resistance. This is despite the fact that most changes are for the better, at least in the long run.

However, change is a constant feature of life and therefore systems need to be in place to manage a continuous process of change which never reaches a stable state. Some commentators have referred to this as 'managing changing' rather than 'managing change'. Organisations with flat structures in which communication is quick and easy have less trouble adapting to change than organisations with hierarchical structures where communication takes a great deal of time and passes through several layers before it reaches the recipients. The key to using internal marketing to manage change is to ensure that the communication lines are kept open and efficient. Intranet systems, open-door policies and open meetings are all useful in defusing the problems that arise from change.

Communication with and from senior management is extremely important because of the way people process information. In the absence of solid information, the human brain has the facility to formulate hypotheses that will be used as a model for the universe until accurate information can be gained. In corporate terms, this means that lack of information about forthcoming changes will result in guesswork by staff, a flood of rumours and even staff actions based on the rumours and hypotheses. At this point, managerial attempts to 'scotch' the rumours are likely to be met with further suspicion. Figure 4.2 shows situations in which senior management needs to provide information to employees, both to allay their fears and to promote more positive attitudes to the change.

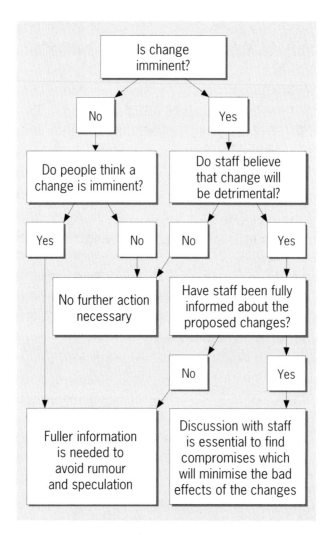

Figure 4.2 *Providing information about change*

Front-line staff

Front-line staff are those who have regular contact with people outside the organisation. These people have an obvious responsibility for public relations and are therefore likely to be key targets for internal marketing activities.

Typical examples of front-line staff are:

♦ receptionists

♦ telephonists

♦ truck drivers

♦ some warehouse staff

♦ serving staff in company canteens

♦ credit controllers

♦ progress chasers.

This list does not include marketing professionals such as salespeople and PR officers whose main role is dealing with people outside the organisation.

Front-line staff have a particular responsibility for maintaining good relationships with the outside world. Although many organisations pay attention to the effect that their receptionists and telephonists have, relatively few pay attention to training their truck drivers in dealing with the public. In recent years it has become fashionable for organisations to have a 'freefone' telephone number on the backs of their trucks so that other road users are able to comment on the driver's road manners, but this does not always extend to ensuring that drivers are polite and helpful when actually making deliveries.

Aer Lingus

During late 1999, Aer Lingus ran a series of magazine advertisements in which it emphasised the friendliness of its staff. Much was said in the advertising about the warm welcome that Irish people traditionally give to strangers, but the most telling point was the headline: 'We don't spend money teaching people to smile at our customers. We just hire nice people to begin with.'

The Aer Lingus example makes a nice story, but in fact life is not that simple. Even nice people have a bad day sometimes or do not know what power they have to make redress in the event of a problem with a customer, and most nice people still need to be trained in dealing with customer complaints or abuse. This is part of the role of internal marketing.

Southwest Airlines

Southwest Airlines has an unusual approach to its customers. For one thing, the company encourages staff to have fun while working – a playful approach to the job is encouraged, and staff will joke with passengers and even play practical jokes on occasion. Also, Southwest takes the attitude that staff morale is essential to good customer relations – unlike most organisations, the airline takes pride in saying that staff morale comes ahead of customer service. As a result, the company claims that customer service is actually improved – because staff are better motivated and happier, they present a more positive face to the customers.

Embedded within the corporate culture is the notion that business effectiveness depends upon the ability to build strong and caring relationships between staff members. Regardless of position or title, employees are expected to be available to one another, and the company operates a culture committee to ensure that this happens. One culture committee member shared some interesting comments from a senior manager:

'While I was out in the field visiting one of our stations, one of the managers mentioned to me that he wanted to put up a suggestion box. And I responded to him by saying, "Sure, why don't you put up a suggestion box right here on the wall and admit you are a failure as a manager?" Our theory at Southwest is, if you have to put up a box so people can write down their ideas and toss them in, then it means you are not doing what you are supposed to do. You are supposed to be setting your people up to be winners. To do that you should be listening to them and available to them in person, not via a suggestion box. And, for the most part, I think that most people employed here know that they can call any one of our vice-presidents on the telephone and get heard, almost immediately. We need to spend at least a third of our time out of the office, walking around. When I do go out in the field, I am much more likely to find that some of the decisions I've made are stupid decisions, and I've seen how my decisions have terribly affected and inconvenienced some of our people. And they definitely pay you with some kind of currency, and if you are incapable of changing things or fixing things or simply doing a self-audit, if you consistently try to sell your employees something they don't want, then what your employees are going to do is fire you! And the problem is, some managers have been fired and don't even know it! But their people won't do business with them any more. They go around them, they're not as committed, and they don't have as much energy. When that happens, our culture is in trouble.'

This approach to communications within the company sounds like a recipe for disaster. The managers are apparently going to be spending a great deal of their time listening to complaints from employees and even more time in trying to elicit comment from the staff. In practice, this does not happen – staff feel empowered, and (for the most part) respect the managers' time and do not waste it. Equally, managers try not to waste employees' time, and go to some trouble to ensure that staff are given sufficient leeway to be able to operate effectively.

Activity 11
Managing change

Objective

Use this activity to understand change management in your organisation. The objective is to assess the effectiveness of change management and to identify flaws in the approach. In turn, this should help you learn some lessons for the future and to consider ways in which change management could be handled more effectively.

Task

Consider a recent major change in your organisation. Use the matrix provided to analyse the way the change was handled. Tick the boxes to indicate what you believe was the case – if you like, you could get a friend or colleague to discuss the questions with you as you complete the task to confirm your own impressions of the change management process.

	To a large extent	To an extent	Not much	Not at all
Was the change flagged up to staff in advance?	☐	☐	☐	☐
Was discussion of the change carried out in a formal way?	☐	☐	☐	☐
Did negative rumours about the change circulate among staff?	☐	☐	☐	☐
Did positive rumours about the change circulate among staff?	☐	☐	☐	☐
Did management take action concerning the rumours?	☐	☐	☐	☐
Did any staff lose out as a result of the change?	☐	☐	☐	☐
Did any staff gain noticeably as a result of the change?	☐	☐	☐	☐
Were staff who lost out recompensed in some way?	☐	☐	☐	☐
Was it clear that staff who gained by the change deserved to do so?	☐	☐	☐	☐
Did management gain or lose in credibility as a result of the way the change was handled?	☐	☐	☐	☐

Feedback

You should be able to identify a relationship between the way the change was handled and the effects on the credibility of managers. You should also be able to discern a relationship between the amount of information given by management and the level of rumour which resulted – the less the change was flagged up to staff in advance, the greater the degree of rumour-mongering (especially negative rumours).

Whenever there is change, there will be gainers and losers. The greater the degree to which these gains and losses are seen to be fair, the better the effect on management credibility (and, of course, on staff morale).

◆ Recap

Consider why it is important to manage the internal image

◆ Employee attitudes have a considerable impact on the success of the organisation: firstly, in terms of their motivation to do their job and, secondly, as ambassadors for the organisation.

◆ Employers need to encourage their employees to feel proud of their organisation and its work. Employees need to be able to answer questions about how the organisation is doing, where their contribution fits and why it matters.

Explore techniques for managing the internal image

◆ Part of the remit for answering the above questions lies with the internal PR team, who use a mix of PR tools including corporate intranets, staff magazines, internal newsletters and staff meetings to communicate.

◆ Managing the internal image extends beyond communication. Employers need to manage the exchange process with their staff. Important exchanges are:

  – time for salary

  – loyalty for supportive management

  – effort for respect

  – commitment and ideas for information about the organisation's future direction.

Assess the effectiveness of the house journal in your organisation

◆ House journals are a popular means of disseminating information, but they actually do more than this. A well-designed house journal also helps to strengthen the corporate culture and promotes loyalty by marketing key messages and recognising achievement.

◆ Readership, quality, frequency of publication, editorial policy, title, the print process, style and format are all important considerations for a house journal.

Consider how internal marketing can be used to support the change process in organisations

◆ Managing change is a major preoccupation in organisations. An effective flow of information between senior management and employees is critical to prevent staff acting on rumour and hypotheses.

◆ Internal marketing has an important role to play in keeping the communication lines open. Intranets, open-door policies and open meetings are all useful techniques.

▶▶ **More @**

Quirke, B. (2002) *Making the Connections: Using Internal Communication to Turn Strategy into Action*, Gower Publishing
This book looks at what a business needs from its people to succeed, what gets in the way, and the role of communication in helping to bridge the gap.

Holtz, S. (2003) *Corporate Conversations: A Guide to Crafting Effective and Appropriate Internal Communications*, Amacom
This book aims to help companies improve their communication skills and align business correspondence with the corporate message.

The **Chartered Institute of Personnel and Development** publishes employee communication survey information and best practice guides on its website at
www.cipd.co.uk/subjects/empreltns/empcomm. Some areas require subscription but there are many excellent free resources.

Larkin, T. and Larkin, S. (1993) *Communicating Change: Winning Employee Support for New Business Goals*, McGraw-Hill
This book offers specific prescriptions for effecting successful change, centred around three guiding principles: conveying the message through supervisors; communicating face to face; and making the changes relevant to each work area.

5 Managing the external image

This theme explores how an organisation can manage its image with the outside world.

In the days of instant messaging, instant access, and 24/7 news cycles, strong, professionally run public relations operations are critical to the success of the most successful organisations.

> **Next to doing the right thing, the most important thing is to let people know you are doing the right thing.**
> **John D. Rockefeller**
> **Oil magnate and philanthropist, (1839–1937)**

You start by considering the strategic role of public relations in influencing how the public views your organisation.

You then go on to explore the topic of corporate governance and how ethical behaviour and meeting legal responsibilities play an increasing part in the creation and destruction of corporate image and reputation.

Organisations face crises all the time – product recalls, plant closures, a crime committed by an employee, a company leader making a poor personal decision. The fact that we only hear a selection of stories of this kind in the media illustrates the power of effective crisis communications. In the final part of this book you look at what organisations can do to protect their reputation and image when things go wrong.

You will:

- ◆ Consider how public relations activities help in generating and managing reputation

- ◆ Assess the effectiveness of your organisation's press releases

- ◆ Understand the ethical problems that inform good corporate citizenship and explore ways to improve the ethical stance of the organisation

- ◆ Identify how you can protect your organisation's image and reputation in the event of a corporate crisis.

Public relations and external communication

Public relations or PR is the management of corporate reputation through the management of relationships with the organisation's publics. Roger Haywood (1998) offers an alternative definition:

> ...those efforts used by management to identify and close any gap between how the organisation is seen by its key publics and how it would like to be seen.

What public relations does

PR has more than just a role in defending the organisation from attack and publicising its successes. It has a key role in relationship marketing, since it is concerned with building a long-term reputation rather than gaining a quick sale. There is a strategic relationship between publicity, PR and press relations. PR occupies the overall strategic role in the relationship, as shown in Figure 5.1.

Figure 5.1 *Publicity, PR and press relations*

In some cases, organisations use PR solely for crisis management, either by employing somebody with a nice smile and a friendly voice to handle complaints or by waiting for things to go wrong and then beginning to formulate a plan for handling the problem. This is a firefighting, or reactive, approach to public relations, and is generally regarded as being far less effective than a proactive approach, which seeks to avoid problems arising.

What do public relations managers do?

PR managers have the task of co-ordinating all those activities which make up the public face of the organisation and will have some or all of the following tasks to handle:

- organising press conferences
- organising staff training workshops
- organising social events
- handling incoming complaints or criticism
- grooming senior management for TV or press interviews
- moulding the internal culture of the organisation.

PR people talk about 'publics' rather than 'the public'. This is because they deal with a wide range of people, all with different needs and preconceptions.

Dealing with the following publics may be part of the PR manager's remit:

- customers
- suppliers
- staff
- government and government departments
- local government
- neighbours
- local residents
- the general public
- pressure groups such as environmentalists or trade unions
- other industry members.

In each case the approach will be different and the expected outcomes will also be different. The basic routes by which PR operates are word of mouth, press and TV news stories, and personal recommendation. The aim of good PR is to put the name of the organisation and its products and services into people's minds in a positive way.

PR is not advertising because the organisation does not directly pay for it. Also, advertising can be both informative and persuasive, but PR can only be used for conveying information or for placing the organisation in the public eye in a positive way. PR does not generate business directly, but achieves the organisation's long-term objectives by creating positive feelings. The ideal is to give the world the impression that this is 'a good firm to do business with'.

Tools of public relations

PR people use a number of different ways to achieve their aims. The list in Table 5.1 is by no means comprehensive, but does cover the main tools available to PR managers.

Tool	Description and examples
Press releases	A press release is a news story about the organisation, usually designed to present the organisation in a good light but often intended just to keep it in the public eye. For example, a company might issue a press release about opening a new factory in a depressed area of the country; newspapers print this as news, since it is about creating jobs
Sponsorship	Sponsorship of events, individuals or organisations is useful for creating favourable publicity. For example, Mars sponsored the London Marathon for many years, gaining two or three hours of TV exposure for the brand in exchange for a relatively small outlay
Publicity stunts	Sometimes organisations will stage an event specifically for the purpose of creating a news story. For example, a taxi firm might take a group of deprived children for a day at the seaside, using the firm's cars; this might be sufficiently newsworthy to make the local TV news
Word of mouth	Generating favourable word of mouth is an important aim of PR. For example, Body Shop requires all its franchises to carry out some project to benefit their local community. Inevitably this generates favourable attitudes locally, which enhances Body Shop's reputation as a good corporate citizen
Corporate advertising	Corporate advertising is aimed at improving the corporate image rather than selling products. Examples are the Christmas greetings advertisements put out by major companies such as BT or Tesco on Christmas Day
Lobbying	Lobbying is the process of making representations to members of Parliament or other politicians. For example, an industry association might lobby MPs to persuade Parliament not to introduce new restrictions on its industry

Table 5.1 *Tools of PR*

Of these, the press release and sponsorship are probably the most important.

A press release is a favourable news story about the organisation that originates from within the organisation itself. Newspapers and magazines earn their money mainly through paid advertising, but they attract readers by having stimulating articles about topics of interest to the readership. Editors need to fill space and are quite happy to use a press release to do so if the story is newsworthy and interesting to the readership. Some magazines and newspapers would find it difficult to function without press releases, since they do not have a large enough reporting staff to write all the content.

The advantages of writing a press release are that it is much more credible than an advertisement, it is much more likely to be read and the space within the publication is free. There are, of course, costs attached to producing press releases.

Table 5.2 shows the criteria under which the press stories must be produced if they are to be published. Increasing consumer scepticism and resistance to advertising has meant that there has been a substantial growth in the use of press releases and publicity in recent years. Press stories are much more credible, and although they do not usually generate business directly, they do have a positive long-term effect in building brand awareness and loyalty.

Criterion	Example
Stories must be newsworthy, i.e. of interest to the reader	Articles about your new lower prices are not newsworthy; articles about opening a new factory creating 200 jobs are
Stories must not be merely thinly disguised advertisements	A story saying that your new computer package is great value at only £799 would not be published; a story saying that you were sponsoring a computer literacy campaign in a deprived area would stand a much better chance
Stories must fit the editorial style of the magazine or newspaper to which they are sent	An article sent to *Cosmopolitan* magazine about your new sports car would probably not be published; an article about your new female marketing director probably would

Table 5.2 *Criteria for successful press releases*

Editors do not have to publish press releases exactly as they are received. They reserve the right to alter stories, add to them, comment on them or otherwise change them around to suit their own purposes. For example, a press release about your company's new computer game might turn into part of an article about the damage computer gaming is doing to the nation's youth. There is nothing substantial that press officers can do about this. Cultivating a good relationship with the media is therefore an important part of the press officer's job.

Sometimes this will involve business entertaining, but more often the press officer will simply try to see to it that the job of the press is made as easy as possible. This means supplying accurate and complete information, writing press releases so that they require a minimum of editing and rewriting, and making the appropriate corporate spokesperson available when required.

When business entertaining is appropriate, it will often come as part of a media event or press conference. This may be called to launch a new product, to announce some major corporate development such as a merger or takeover or (less often) when there has been a corporate crisis. This will involve inviting journalists from the appropriate media, serving refreshments and providing corporate spokespeople to answer questions and make statements. This kind of event will have limited success, however, unless the groundwork for it has been thoroughly laid.

Journalists are often suspicious of media events, sometimes feeling that the organisers are trying to buy them off with a buffet and a glass of wine. This means they may not respond positively to the message the PR people are trying to convey, and may write a critical article rather than the positive one that had been hoped for.

To minimise the chance of this happening, media events should follow these basic rules:

- ◆ Avoid calling a media event or press conference unless you are announcing something that the press will find interesting

- ◆ Check that there are no negative connotations in what you are announcing

- ◆ Ensure that you have some of the organisation's senior executives there to talk to the press, not just the PR people

- ◆ Only invite journalists with whom you feel you have a good working relationship

- ◆ Avoid being too lavish with the refreshments

- ◆ Ensure that your senior executives, in fact anybody who is going to speak to the press, has had some training for this – this is particularly important for TV

- ◆ Be prepared to answer all questions truthfully – journalists are trained to spot lies and evasions

- ◆ Take account of the fact that newspapers and the broadcast media have deadlines to which they must adhere – call the conference at a time that will allow reporters enough time to file their stories.

From the press viewpoint, it is always better to speak to the most senior managers available rather than to the PR people. Having said that, senior managers will need some training in handling the press and answering questions, and also need to be fully briefed on anything the press might want to ask. In the case of a press conference called as a result of a crisis, this can be a problem. Many major organisations establish crisis teams of appropriate senior managers who are available and prepared to comment should the need arise. Press officers should be prepared to handle queries from journalists promptly, honestly and enthusiastically, and to arrange interviews with senior personnel if necessary.

Activity 12
Press releases

Objective

Use this activity to assess the effectiveness of your organisation's press releases. The purpose of this exercise is to enable you to consider ways of improving the organisation's success rate with the news media and thus its corporate reputation. The exercise should also help you to consider what makes a good press release and how best to manage the exchanges between the organisation and the media.

Task

Obtain copies of news reports about your organisation. If you are unable to do this, you might be able to find copies of reports about another organisation. If possible, ask your press office or PR manager for copies of press releases which were not published. Many organisations put their press releases on their websites; if possible, obtain copies of the periodicals in which the press releases were ultimately published.

Now use the table provided to rate the press releases. Give each press release points out of 10 for each of the criteria.

Story	Newsworthiness	Fit with editorial style (if you were able to obtain copies of the periodicals)	Avoidance of an advertising style of phraseology

Story	Newsworthiness	Fit with editorial style (if you were able to obtain copies of the periodicals)	Avoidance of an advertising style of phraseology

Feedback

You will probably have found that the press releases scored high on newsworthiness and on fit with the style of the journal. If this were not the case, the story would probably not have been accepted in the first place.

You may have found that the story also avoids advertising-type phraseology. This usually means that there are few adjectives in the story and that the products, brands and even the organisation are not mentioned until well into the story – typically the third or fourth paragraph.

If you were able to obtain copies of unsuccessful (unpublished) press releases, you will almost certainly have found that the stories scored lower on these factors. In some cases, the stories might not have been published because they were knocked off the front page by a major world event, however.

Ethics and corporate responsibility

Public accountability has steadily increased throughout the 20th century and during the early 21st century. Organisations are now expected to conduct their affairs in the full glare of publicity and are held to be accountable for their actions. The public's power to compel organisations to act in ethical ways is exercised almost daily through the use of websites, newspaper reports, boycotts and even litigation.

Ethical theory

Ethics are the principles that define right and wrong. Ethical theory divides into the teleological theories, which state that acts should be defined as right or wrong according to the outcome of the acts, and the deontological approach, which states that acts can be defined as right or wrong regardless of the outcome. Teleology appears to imply that the end justifies the means and that a crime which does not succeed is no crime. Deontology implies that acts themselves can be defined as right or wrong, regardless of who performs the act. This means that something that is wrong for an individual is wrong for a government or a corporation. The deontological approach is illustrated by Kant's Categorical Imperative which states that each act must be based on reasons that anyone could act on, and that decisions to act must be based on reasons that the decision maker would accept for others to use in justifying their actions. In simple terms, this means that what is sauce for the goose is sauce for the gander.

In practice, of course, both approaches are fraught with difficulties. According to Kant, an 18th-century philosopher, if it is immoral for an individual to perform an act, it is also immoral for a government to perform it; yet many acts which are legal for governments are illegal for private citizens – going to war being an obvious example. In the corporate world, it is perfectly legal for an individual to run up debts with little or no prospect of being able to repay them, but such behaviour on the part of an organisation carries the death sentence for the organisation. Teleology is equally complex – to say that the end justifies the means opens the door to all sorts of skulduggery in the name of preserving jobs, shareholders' investments or even directors' perquisites.

The basis of corporate ethics is often the prevailing ethics of society at large. Corporations are sometimes established according to the religious or ethical stance of the founders (for example, Rowntree was founded as a model company run on Quaker principles) but often the moral code is expedient, based on prevailing attitudes. For example, most mission statements nowadays seem to contain a statement about environmentalism and virtually all contain a commitment to staff development, but these statements are frequently empty. Business is not inherently immoral, of course. The visionaries who founded some of the UK's most successful organisations did so by using a combination of firm ethical principles and solid business sense.

The ethical stance of an organisation is likely to attract people who have similar ethical principles, but research shows that most people have separate sets of morals for business and private life. Obviously the closer the organisation's ethical position is to that of its employees, the less likelihood there is of dissonance, therefore managers would be well advised to draw up a code of conduct to which employees feel they can subscribe. Organisations need to have a code of practice, and to monitor the code in practice, so that all stakeholders (and indeed outsiders) know what the organisation intends to do about its ethical responsibilities.

Establishing a corporate ethical framework

The starting point for any corporate ethical framework is likely to be the mission statement. Over the past 20 years or so it has become fashionable for organisations to have a mission statement in which it lays down clearly where it thinks the organisation is going and what kind of organisation it is intended to be. This is largely for strategic purposes, to ensure that everyone within the organisation is heading in the same direction and has a blueprint against which they are able to judge their actions.

Unfortunately, many mission statements are simply hollow rhetoric, intended to cover senior management's true intentions. Because there is a strong view that every organisation should have one, mission statements are drawn up without sufficient thought as to how they might be implemented, with the result that the ringing phrases and high moral tone of the statement are never actually put into practice. Table 5.3 shows the elements of a good mission statement.

> At this moment, America's highest economic need is higher ethical standards – standards enforced by strict rules and upheld by responsible business leaders
>
> **George Bush, US President, 2002**

Element	Description
Purpose	Why the organisation exists. Organisations do not necessarily exist purely to make a profit. For most founders of organisations, and indeed for most boards of directors, organisations exist to achieve something which senior management feels is really worth doing. Profit is what enables such organisations to stay in the game
Strategy	The organisation's competitive position and distinctive competence. This is the statement of how the organisation expects to distinguish itself from organisations offering similar benefits to customers
Behaviour standards	Norms and rules – 'the way we do things round here'. Behaviour standards will include the way customers are dealt with and the way staff are treated
Values	These are the moral principles and beliefs that underpin the behaviour standards. Normally these values will first have been put in place by the founders or by the directors, but sometimes they will have grown up empirically over the life of the organisation

Table 5.3 *Elements of the mission*

Pressure groups

Pressure groups such as environmentalists or local associations are clearly a factor in controlling corporate excesses. Sometimes organisations will try to use advertising to counter adverse publicity from pressure groups, but the success rate is limited.

McDonald's and the rainforests

McDonald's was attacked by environmental groups for indirectly encouraging the destruction of rainforests for the purpose of producing cheap beef. McDonald's responded with a series of full-page press adverts proving that beef for its hamburgers comes only from sources within the countries where they are eaten and is not imported from the Third World.

These advertisements had limited success because they actually attracted attention to the environmentalists' claims, which up until then had been fairly low-profile due to lack of resources. Environmentalists continued to lobby and issue statements, some of which were actually untrue. McDonald's fought a successful libel action against one group, but again this backfired because it was seen as an example of a large corporation going after the little guy. Again, the case was widely publicised, which gave greater circulation to those anti-McDonald's statements which were true.

Of course, despite the fact that McDonald's is regularly attacked by pressure groups, the company still remains the world's largest and most popular restaurant group – so perhaps bad publicity is not as harmful as might be supposed.

Most journalists will make an honest effort to get both sides of the story, so when approached by a pressure group they will try to contact the organisation concerned. This is partly for legal reasons, to avoid libel accusations if the story is untrue, but also most journalists are professionals and prefer to write accurate and fair stories. This means that an organisation's press office, a PR manager or even a senior executive may be asked for comment with little or no prior warning, which can prove stressful to say the least.

Managers who find themselves in this position should try to avoid appearing evasive. It is better to use an expression such as, 'I'm sorry, I'll have to look into that and get back to you,' rather than to say, 'No comment'. The former at least gives the impression that you are trying to help, whereas 'No comment' gives the impression that you are trying to hide something.

The 'No comment' approach is an example of defensive PR, which is an approach whereby managers respond to attacks from outside the organisation and counteract them as they arise. The safest way to handle this type of attack is to begin by trying to understand the enemy, and to this end the following questions should be asked:

1 Are they justified in their criticism?

2 What facts do they have at their disposal?

3 Who are they trying to influence?

4 How are they trying to do it?

Pressure groups are often justified in their criticisms and can bring evidence to bear to prove their claims. As with a complaint from a dissatisfied customer, the pressure group may be giving the organisation a last chance to correct the problem before taking matters further. In these circumstances it might be necessary to encourage the organisation to make any necessary changes rather than risk a PR disaster.

Most authors consider a proactive approach to pressure groups to be a safer course of action because it leads to fewer surprise calls from journalists. In the proactive case, managers need to decide the following:

1 Who to influence.

2 What to influence them about.

3 How to influence them.

4 How to marshal the arguments carefully to maximise the impact.

Consulting the possible pressure groups before implementing a proposed course of action is almost certainly going to be cheaper and easier than waiting for problems to arise. Often the relevant groups can be helpful in deciding on a course of action that will be seen as ethical, and will sometimes hold the organisation up as an example of good practice.

Professional ethics for public relations officers

The Arthur W. Page Society, a US organisation of public relations professionals, has the following principles enshrined in its constitution:

♦ Tell the truth. Let the public know what's happening and provide an accurate picture of the company's character, ideals and practices.

♦ Prove it with action. Public perception of an organisation is determined ninety per cent by doing and ten per cent by talking.

♦ Listen to the customer. To serve the company well, understand what the public wants and needs. Keep top decision makers and other employees informed about public reaction to company products, policies and practices.

♦ Manage for tomorrow. Anticipate public reaction and eliminate practices that create difficulties. Generate goodwill.

♦ Conduct public relations as if the whole company depends on it. Corporate relations are a management function. No corporate strategy should be implemented without considering its impact on the public. The public relations professional is a policymaker capable of handling a wide range of corporate communications activities.

♦ Remain calm, patient and good-humoured. Lay the groundwork for public relations miracles with consistent, calm and reasoned attention to information and contacts. When a crisis arises, remember that cool heads communicate best.

Source: *Arthur W. Page Society*

Such codes of ethics enable professionals to ensure that their actions are ethical and give them a yardstick against which they can control their daily activities.

Activity 13
Ethical analysis

Objective

Use this activity to assess some of the ethical issues surrounding your organisation's activities. The purpose of this activity is to compare the ethical stance of the organisation with your own ethical stance. This should help you to consider ways of closing the gap between the corporate ethics and the ethics of the employees, and also to consider the nature of the contract between employees and the organisation. To what extent can employees be expected to adopt the ethical stance of the organisation, and vice versa?

Task

Use the table provided to make a list of the activities your organisation is involved in. Next to each activity, indicate whether the activity is ethical, neutral or unethical according to your own code of ethics.

Activity	Ethical	Neutral	Unethical
	☐	☐	☐
	☐	☐	☐
	☐	☐	☐
	☐	☐	☐
	☐	☐	☐
	☐	☐	☐
	☐	☐	☐
	☐	☐	☐
	☐	☐	☐
	☐	☐	☐
	☐	☐	☐
	☐	☐	☐

Can you explain your answers? Why do you feel that some of the corporate activities are immoral? Who is affected by these activities? Why did you accept (or even assist with) carrying out activities which you think are unethical?

Your assessment:

Feedback

Most organisations do things which some of their employees might regard as unethical. This does not prevent them from becoming involved in the process, or even helping with it.

You may have reconciled this internal conflict by accepting that not everyone's view is the same, and what is unethical for some people is acceptable to others. You may have reconciled the conflict by changing your own ethical stance. You may have reconciled it by thinking that the end justifies the means. You may even have changed your view of the organisation.

Finally, though, you may decide that you cannot reconcile the problem, and you have no alternative but to look for a job elsewhere. This is a rare, but not unknown, solution to this type of ethical dissonance.

Protecting reputation and image: risk management

Life is risky. Business life is also risky, and managers need to be aware of this when organising their crisis management contingency plans.

No matter how carefully PR activities are planned and prepared for, crises will develop from time to time. Preparing for the unexpected is therefore a necessity. Some PR agencies specialise in crisis management, but a degree of advance preparation will certainly help if the worst should happen. Preparing for a crisis is similar to organising a fire drill: the fire may never happen, but it is as well to be prepared.

Crises may be very likely to happen, or extremely unlikely. For example, most manufacturing firms can expect to have a product-related problem sooner or later, and either need to recall products for safety reasons or need to make adaptations to future versions of the product. On the other hand, some crises are extremely unlikely. Assassination or kidnapping of senior executives is not common in most parts of the world, nor are products rendered illegal without considerable warning beforehand.

> **While no one can predict a crisis, appropriate foresight and thought can mean the difference between maintaining a stellar corporate reputation and the dreadful alternative.**
>
> **Abbe Ruttenberg Serphos, ABR Communications**

Crises can also be defined as either within the organisation's control or outside the organisation's control. Many organisations have been beset by problems which were really not of their making. A classic example is that of Pan American Airlines (Pan Am) which, as the US flag-carrying airline, was regularly attacked by terrorist groups, culminating in the Lockerbie disaster in which a Pan Am 747 was destroyed over a Scottish village in 1988. In the aftermath of this disaster, Pan Am found itself unable to sell seats, and eventually the company went bankrupt.

In fact, Pan Am had systems in place for coping with terrorist bomb threats. The problem was that the company received an average of four such threats every day, virtually all of which proved to be hoaxes. If the airline had grounded its aircraft every time a threat was received, no Pan Am plane would ever have flown.

Pan Am further compounded the problem by failing to handle the crisis well from a PR perspective – the company was seen to be uncaring and somewhat heartless in its dealings with victims' families and did not at first admit to having had a terrorist warning that a bomb was on board the plane.

Very few problems are entirely outside the organisation's control. In most cases, events can at least be influenced, if not controlled.

Sometimes, however, the cost of such influence is out of all proportion to the level of risk involved. Figure 5.2 shows the elements involved in good crisis management.

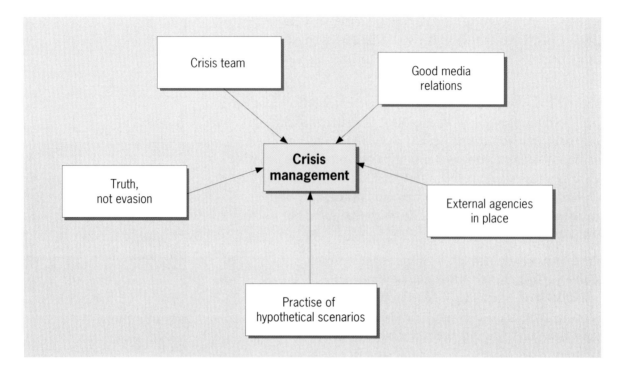

Figure 5.2 *Elements of good crisis management*

Establishing a crisis team

Ideally, the organisation should establish a permanent crisis management team of perhaps four or five individuals who are able to take decisions and act as spokespeople in the event of a crisis. Typical members might be the personnel manager, the safety officer, the factory manager, the PR officer and at least one member of the board of directors. Keeping the crisis team small means that communication between members is easy and fast.

The team should meet regularly to review potential risks and formulate strategies for dealing with crises. It may even be possible to rehearse responses in the case of the most likely crises. Importantly, the team should be trained in presentation techniques for dealing with the media, especially in the event of a TV interview.

The team should be able to contact each other immediately in the event of a crisis and should also be provided with deputies in case any members are away on business, on holiday, off sick or otherwise unavailable when a crisis occurs. The essence of planning for crises is to have as many fallback positions as possible; the need to have a Plan B is obvious, but it is wise to have a Plan C or even Plan D as well.

Dealing with the media in a crisis

One of the main PR problems inherent in crisis management is the fact that many crises are newsworthy. This means that reporters will be attracted to the organisation and its officers in the hope of getting comments or newsworthy statements which will help to sell newspapers.

Provided the groundwork has been laid, the organisation should already have a good relationship with the news media. This will help in the event of a crisis. However, many managers still feel a degree of trepidation when facing the press at a crisis news conference. The journalists are not there to help the organisation out of a crisis; they are there to hunt down (or create) a story. Their objectives are probably not compatible with those of the organisation, but they are under an obligation to report the news reasonably accurately.

Preparation is important. As soon as the crisis breaks, the crisis team should be ready to organise a press conference, preferably on the organisation's territory. The press conference should be held as soon as is reasonably possible, but the team should allow the spokespeople sufficient time to prepare themselves for the journalists and give a reasonable excuse for not talking to reporters ahead of time. The crisis team members should remember that they are in charge. It is their information, their crisis and their story. They are not under an obligation to the news media, but they are under an obligation to the organisation's shareholders, customers, employees and other publics. The media may or may not be helpful in communicating with these publics in a crisis situation.

Another important consideration is to ensure that the situation is not made worse by careless statements. Insurance and legal liability may be affected by anything that is said, so all statements should be checked beforehand.

Eurolines

In the summer of 1999, a Eurolines bus en route from Warsaw to London was involved in an accident with a lorry while driving through Germany. Many passengers were injured, some seriously, and the bus company was faced with a potential PR crisis even though the accident was not the fault of the Eurolines driver.

The injured passengers were taken straight to a hospital in Germany to be treated and Eurolines' German agents compiled a list of passengers which also identified the injured. Those passengers who were fit enough were offered free telephone facilities so that they could notify their friends and families of the incident and reassure them of their safety. The passenger list was immediately sent to the Eurolines' office at Victoria Coach Station in London so that waiting friends and relatives could have up-to-date information regarding the passengers. Eurolines' London staff took telephone numbers of those waiting so that they could be notified of any changes in circumstances, and a hotline was set up for worried relatives to call for information.

Some of the passengers were too severely injured to be moved, but the majority were able to travel. They were offered the choice of returning to Warsaw or of continuing on to London on a second bus sent to Germany specifically for the purpose. Family and friends waiting in London were notified which of the options each passenger had taken. Since the second bus would be arriving in the small hours of the morning, the passengers would be accommodated at a five-star hotel near the bus station. Those waiting to meet the passengers were offered three options: to stay at the hotel, to go home and be called the next day or to have their friends 'delivered' by Eurolines or National Express coaches the following day, at Eurolines' expense.

At the hotel, Eurolines' emergency team was set up. The team consisted of senior Eurolines managers, a medical team, interpreters for Polish, Lithuanian, Russian and other language groups known to be on the bus, and a team of administrators briefed to arrange onward transportation and emergency help for people whose luggage was scattered along a German autobahn. As the passengers limped or were wheeled in they were offered sandwiches, tea and coffee and the opportunity for medical treatment and other assistance. Most of them continued straight to bed after a long and exhausting day. The location of the hotel was kept secret from the press. This was not particularly difficult to do since the accident was only really newsworthy in Germany, where it had happened.

The following morning, Eurolines staff were available both at the hotel and at the company's offices to offer any further assistance. Passengers and those meeting them were offered exemplary service, including free coach tickets to any UK location, access to embassy consular services and ongoing medical treatment for those needing it. Eventually, once the accident enquiry was completed in Germany, the passengers also received substantial compensation. All those involved, whether as passengers or as friends and relatives of passengers, were delighted with the way Eurolines handled the crisis. What was potentially a PR disaster was turned into a PR victory by the professional way the crisis was handled – despite the fact that Eurolines rarely have the opportunity to put these skills into practice.

Crisis teams need to have a special set of talents, as well as the training needed to perform their ordinary jobs. Rapid communication and rapid response are essential when the crisis occurs. Good relationships with the news media will pay off in times of crisis.

Crisis management should not be left until the crisis happens. Everyone involved should be briefed beforehand on what the crisis policy is. This enables everyone to respond appropriately, without committing the organisation to inappropriate actions – in simple terms, being prepared for a crisis will help to prevent panic reactions and over-hasty responses which might come back to haunt the organisation later.

Activity 14
Establishing a crisis team

Objective

Use this activity to consider how to establish a crisis team in your organisation. The purpose of this exercise is to help you consider the types of crisis which might affect your organisation, and thus the particular individuals who would be most effective in dealing with the crisis. These individuals are not necessarily the most senior in the organisation. This exercise should also focus your thinking on the possible training and support these people would need in advance of a crisis.

Task

1 Use the table provided to list the possible types of crisis which might befall your organisation. Be imaginative – the point about a crisis is that it is unusual!

Crisis 1

Crisis 2

Crisis 3

Crisis 4	
Crisis 5	

2 Then, in the second table, list the departments that might need to become involved in handling that type of crisis.

Within each department, you should be able to identify appropriate individuals who would possess the necessary expertise and knowledge to be able to handle the crisis. Such individuals should have the following characteristics:

♦ They should be team workers

♦ They should have been with the organisation long enough to understand the corporate vision and objectives

♦ They should have a good network of contacts within the organisation

♦ They should have sufficient formal authority, or sufficient respect within their departments, to be able to push decisions through.

List these individuals in the right-hand column of the table.

	Departments involved	Individuals with necessary skills and knowledge
Crisis 1		
Crisis 2		

	Departments involved	Individuals with necessary skills and knowledge
Crisis 3		
Crisis 4		
Crisis 5		

Feedback

You will almost certainly have found that some departments and individuals feature frequently in the table you have drawn up. The ones who feature most frequently are the ones who should be formed into the crisis team.

There should also be a cut-off point, however. In some cases there will be people who only feature once in your list; although you may feel that it is desirable to include such people in your team, you need to decide whether it is likely that they will be needed for dealing with most of the possible crises. Obviously some crises are more likely to occur than others, so there is little point in including someone on the crisis team who would rarely be called upon to act.

◆ Recap

Consider how public relations activities help in generating and managing reputation

◆ PR plays a strategic role in relationship marketing and is concerned with building the long-term reputation of the organisation with the organisation's publics. It extends beyond the tactical tools of publicity and press relations.

◆ The tools used by PR include press releases, sponsorship, publicity stunts, word-of-mouth, corporate advertising and lobbying.

Assess the effectiveness of your organisation's press releases

◆ Press releases are stories about the organisation, published in newspapers, posted on the Internet or broadcast on television and radio. Press releases are produced in order to communicate values about the organisation and to enhance its reputation.

◆ There are three criteria for a successful press release: the story must be newsworthy, it should not be a thinly veiled advertisement and it must fit with the editorial style of the paper or magazine to which you are sending it.

Understand the ethical problems that inform good corporate citizenship and explore ways to improve the ethical stance of the organisation

◆ In some cases the corporate ethical stance will conflict with the ethical stances of the organisation's employees. There is evidence that people are able to adopt one ethical stance in their personal lives and an entirely different stance in their professional lives.

◆ An organisation needs to have an ethical framework that explains to its stakeholders what it intends to do about its ethical responsibilities. This might be captured in a mission statement or presented as a separate code of practice.

Identify how you can protect your organisation's image and reputation in the event of a corporate crisis

◆ Organisations should regularly assess potential risks to their reputation and image and have contingency plans in place for dealing with crises.

◆ Having good media relations, established relationships with external agencies, practising hypothetical scenarios, being truthful and having a crisis team in place are all elements of good crisis management.

◆ A crisis team is a group of people within the organisation whose purpose is to provide a coherent corporate response to a potential public relations crisis.

▶▶ More @

Branson, R. (Foreword), Barry, A. (2002) *PR Power: Inside Secrets from the World of Spin*, **Virgin Business Guides**
Find out why some of the world's most successful entrepreneurs, such as Jeff Bezos, Anita Roddick and Stelios Haji-Ioannou, view PR with a passion.

Larkin, J. (2002) *Strategic Reputation Risk Management,* **Palgrave-MacMillan**
This book provides practical models and checklists designed to plan reputation management and risk communication strategies.

Neef, D. (2003) *Managing Corporate Reputation and Risk: Developing a Strategic Approach to Corporate Integrity Using Knowledge Management*, **Butterworth-Heinemann**

The **American Marketing Association** provides articles and webcasts to improve your public relations – www.marketingpower.com/topics13.php

www.knowthis.com is another online marketing portal – the **Marketing Virtual Library**. Use 'public relations' to search.

References

The American Marketing Association, www.marketingpower.com.

Arthur W. Page Society, www.awpagesociety.com

Balmer, J. (Editor) and Greyser, S. (Editor) (2003) *Revealing the Corporation: Perspectives on Identity, Image, Reputation and Corporate Branding,* Routledge

Black, A., Wright, P. and Bachman, J. E. (1998) *In Search of Shareholder Value,* Pitman Publishing

Blythe, J. (1997) *Essence of Consumer Behaviour,* Prentice Hall Europe

Branson, R. (Foreword) and Barry, A. (2002) *PR Power: Inside Secrets from the World of Spin,* Virgin Business Guides

The Chartered Institute of Personnel and Development www.cipd.co.uk/subjects/empreltns/empcomm

Cordeiro, J. J. and Sambharya, R. (1997) 'Do corporate reputations influence security analyst earnings forecasts?', *Corporate Reputation Review,* Vol. 1, No. 2, pp. 94–98

Davies, G., Chun, R., Vinhas Da Silva, R. and Roper, S. (2002) *Corporate Reputation and Competitiveness,* Routledge

D'Apris, R. quoted in Arnott, M. 'Effective Employee Communication' in Hart, N. (ed) (1987) *Effective Corporate Relations,* McGraw-Hill

De Chernatony, L. and McDonald, M. (2003) 3nd edition, *Creating powerful brands,* Butterworth-Heinemann

De Geus, A. (1997) *The Living Company,* Harvard Business School Press

Fombrun, C. J. (1996) *Reputation: Realizing Value from the Corporate Image,* Harvard Business School Press

Fombrun, C. J. and Rindova, V. in Schultz, M., Hatch, M. J. and Larsen, M. H. (2000) *The Expressive Organisation,* Oxford University Press

Gordon, W. and Valentine, V. (1996) 'Buying the brand at point of choice', *Journal of Brand Management,* Vol. 4, No. 1, 35–44

Gregory, A. (2000) *Planning and Managing a PR Campaign,* Kogan Page

Harris, T. L. (2000) *Value Added Public Relations,* NTC Publishing

Hayward, R. (1998) *Public Relations for Marketing Professionals,* Macmillan

Haywood, R. (1998) *All About PR,* McGraw-Hill

Hefler, M. (1994) 'Making sure sponsorship meets all the parameters', *Brandweek,* May

Holtz, S. (2003) *Corporate Conversations: A Guide to Crafting Effective and Appropriate Internal Communications*, Amacom

Kanter, R. M. (1985) *The Change Masters – Corporate Entrepreneurs at Work*, Unwin

Larkin, J. (2002) *Strategic Reputation Risk Management*, Palgrave Macmillan

Larkin, T. and Larkin, S. (1993) *Communicating Change: Winning Employee Support for New Business Goals*, McGraw-Hill

The Manchester Business School, www.mbs.ac.uk/research/centres-projects/corporate-reputation/index.htm

Meenaghan, J. A. (1991) 'The role of sponsorship in the marketing communications mix', *International Journal of Advertising,* Vol. 10, Iss. 1, 35–47

Morita, A. (1987) *Made in Japan*, HarperCollins

Neef, D. (2003) *Managing Corporate Reputation and Risk: Developing a Strategic Approach to Corporate Integrity Using Knowledge Management*, Butterworth-Heinemann

Pearson, A. J. (1980) *Setting Corporate Objectives as a Basis for Action*, National Development and Management Foundation of South Aftica

Png, J. P. and Reitmann, D. (1995) 'Why are some products branded and others not?' *Journal of Law and Economics*, Vol. 38, 349–373

Public Relations Consultants' Association, *Getting the Best from a PR Consultancy*, Willow House, Willow Place, Victoria, London SW1P 1JH, United Kingdom

Quirke, B. (2002) *Making the Connections: Using Internal Communication to Turn Strategy into Action*, Gower Publishing

Ries, A. (1995) 'What's in a name?' *Sales and Marketing Management*, October, 36–37

Rossi, P. and Freeman, H. (1999) *Evaluation: A Systematic Approach*, Sage

Schultz, M., Hatch, M. J. and Larsen M. H. (eds) (2000)*The Expressive Organisation*, Oxford University Press

Singh, J. (1988) 'Consumer complaint intention and behaviour: definition and taxonomic issues', *Journal of Marketing*, January, 93–107

Zafer Erdogan, B. and Kitchen, P. J. (1998) 'The interaction between advertising and sponsorship: uneasy alliance or strategic symbiosis?', Proceedings of the 3rd Annual Conference of the Global Institute for Corporate and Marketing Communications, Strathclyde Business School